MW00873821

It's Not That Hard To . . .

A Collection of Personal Essays

by

Faith M. Phillips

For Brad,
What a strange
and beautiful journey.
I'm grateful for our family
for support and love along
the way.
Love, F.M. Phillips

Cover art and photography with permission Copyright ©
2016 by Lavada Nicholls Photography.

Original lyrics published with permission Copyright © 2013
by Steve Ripley.

IT'S NOT THAT HARD TO . . . Copyright © 2016 by Faith
Phillips. All rights reserved. Printed in the United States of
America.

No parts of this book may be used or reproduced in any
manner whatsoever without written permission, except in
the case of brief quotations embodied in critical articles and
reviews.

For more information, contact the author at
www.readbooksby.faith

Geoff Wilson Web Design

Norman, Oklahoma

All rights reserved.

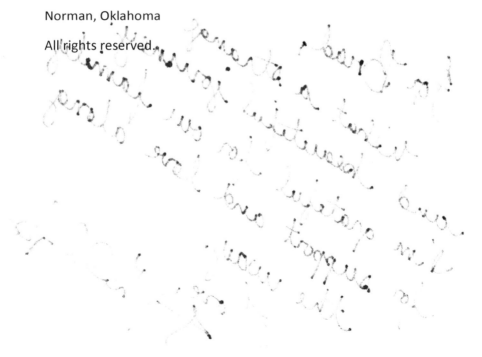

Meet the Phantom Frog Lady of Dornick Hills

My sisters and I amount to an odd jumbling of our parents. We don't look too much alike, though some say a resemblance is found in the eyes. I'm six feet tall and dark blonde, the middle sister, Boog, is 5'2" and brunette. The baby sister, Missy, stands somewhere in between. We're all quite strange, but Missy is by far the strangest.

I've always been quite modest with my body. I admired my confident friends who could walk around stark naked without a stitch, free and unashamed. But I just don't have that in my software. Although skinny-dipping is a different story. Maybe we'll get around to that later.

My best friend lived in a nice house in a prestigious neighborhood located right on a golf course. She was headed out of town for the weekend and asked me to house sit/dog sit/ass sit. Never one to deny myself a chance at padded luxury or bobbing about in a Jacuzzi, I agreed. My baby sister just happened to be in town with her boyfriend, Philip. I invited them over to keep me company that night. We sprawled out in poolside lounge chairs, taking turns playing tunes and telling stories. From a backyard a couple of houses down the way, we heard the unmistakable din of a big party going on. I'd noticed the group gathering earlier in the day, a big stag party for a bunch of golfers who'd just come into town for a tournament. We weren't interested in eavesdropping on their conversation, far from it. But the men spoke loudly, boasting and interrupting, trying their best to one-up each other with stories about a new boat, an investment deal and their best friend's hot new trophy wife. They were annoying, but what could we do about it? We were out of our element. Hillbillies can't call the cops on rich folk, lest they receive the nightstick.

Missy walked in that night wearing a queer crocheted hat, fashioned to look just like a frog. It had eyes sewn on the top and everything. She enjoyed a couple glasses of wine and became increasingly upset with the loud posturing floating in on our peaceful evening. The iron posts that separated the houses from the course were easily spaced eight or so inches apart, so that people sitting in their backyards could view the golfers as they jaunted past during the day. Missy looked at us with a shining gleam in her eye.

"I'm gonna streak 'em," she said.

I was horrified. My thoughts immediately went to my friend, whose house I'd been asked to look after. If she received word that something like *this* occurred in her polite neighborhood on my watch, she might never speak to me again. I imagined the headlines in the local newspaper the next day. "Phillips Girl Arrested for Indecent Exposure in Dornick Hills." I looked to Missy's boyfriend for help in dissuading her, but he only had a look in his eyes that amounted to a mixture of pride, love, delight and great admiration.

I halted my pleas for mercy because she was already pulling off items of clothing. When she was finished she stood there at last in the dim, green glow of the underwater pool lights, absolutely 100%, stark dadgum naked. Except for that frog hat.

She began to climb over to the golf green. The wrought iron fence posts were topped off by little black spear-looking points. I decided I'd better help my sister then, because she was gonna do it anyway, and the only scenario I imagined worse than the one we were already in, was the one in which she became high-centered up there, naked on a spike.

We were all very quiet. Philip and I hoisted her up and over. She landed with a thud on the other side. Outside the faint glow from the pool it was inky black out there. Philip and I just crouched down by the fence, listening. We couldn't see what was happening at all. Too much time went by and I began to fear something had gone terribly wrong. The babel from the golfer party continued, unabated.

But then I heard Missy clear her throat with dramatic effect. The golfer party suddenly fell into a dead silence. She paused for a few seconds, for dramatic effect, I suppose. Then she yelled, "The price is WRONG, BITCH!"

I expected to hear shouts of anger in return.

Outrage. Laughter, perhaps. But, no. Not a single sound came out of those men for a very long time. One of them managed to say at last, in a tone filled with disbelief and considerable terror, "What the hell was *that*?"

Missy used their shocked paralysis as her opportunity to make an escape. She sprinted back to the fence and without uttering a sound we helped her back over, onto the poolside cement. In silence and with one quick motion we scooped up her clothes. Together we ran back into the house, where all three of us collapsed with our faces in the cushions of the couch so the traumatized golfers couldn't hear our laughter.

To this day, I cannot pass a golf course without thinking of those poor men. I wonder if they shudder a bit in their beds from time to time, recalling the night they found

themselves visited by The Phantom Frog Lady of Dornick
Hills.

Be a Capital G

My sister and I drove my dad's old '86 Chevy to high
school every day. I drove, that is, she hated negotiating a
standard. We called it The Bug Truck because it served as his
company vehicle for our small time extermination business.
Boog was considered one of the most beautiful girls in school
and she took great care to maintain that image. Her hair and
makeup were perfect every day, no exceptions. She
meticulously planned her outfits every night before bed.
Boog liked to push the envelope with her style and was sent
home more than once for wearing get-ups that offended the
faculty, including an audacious pair of jeans with faux-leather

patched on the front to make them look like chaps.

The two of us were pretty opposite, socially. All the dudes were interested in her. She had her first boyfriend at age twelve. Many of the other girls were jealous of Boog and regarded her with disdain. But all the girls loved me, and so did the guys – as a friend. My love interests were sparse. I didn't have a boyfriend until I was sixteen, and even then only because a younger guy was brash enough to blatantly express interest.

When Boog and I rode to school we didn't talk much. We mostly jammed out to music, Pearl Jam and Tom Petty, Hole and Alice In Chains. The Rolling Stones. We only turned the music down if one of us had some particularly revelatory statement of dire importance. Neither of us cared for idle chit chat. The road we ran was called England Hollow, although the locals pronounce it "England Holler". It's a tree-lined, twisted and narrow little road. Paved, but in some places it narrows so that two vehicles approaching from opposite directions must play a perilous game of head-on chicken. The drive from home to school was twenty five miles, though it took forty minutes because the road is so treacherous.

We saw many interesting country sights in those few years driving back and forth, but one day beat the hell out of the rest. The road was replete with road kill; coyotes and foxes, dogs and cats, the occasional farm animal. But that day we drove around a corner and lying there in the middle of the road was a solitary severed horse leg. It was an inexplicable sight. No other gore in sight, no blood, no body. Just a leg.

I didn't turn the music down, had no intention of acknowledging a sight that disturbing. I just swung the Bug Truck wide and went right on around the leg. Boog reached out and snapped the radio off.

"Go BACK!" She cried.

It was unusual for her to become so animated. I pulled over at the next available area and questioned her intentions. I am the big sister, after all. She didn't have much to say by way of explanation, but the urgency in her voice made me believe she really needed to go back to the scene of that horror. So I turned around and drove back, irritated at the possibility of arriving late to basketball practice, yet not willing to risk a fight. Little Boog was capable of kicking my big butt when she got worked up.

I sat behind the wheel with the engine running and

told her whatever she had to do, she better be quick about it. Boog hopped out, ran around behind the truck and disappeared from sight behind the tailgate. The next thing I spotted in the rearview mirror was the sight of that hideous leg being hoisted up and over into the bed of the truck. Now, Boog is 5'2" and slender, but the girl is muscular. She competed on a national level in the 220 meter run. She has the body of a sprinter and holds strength uncommon to many women. I've seen her take down many a cocky teenaged boy and some grown men in arm wrestling contests. So, it came as no surprise that she could lift that leg. The concern was, of course, *why* she lifted the leg. We would go to school with a severed leg in the back of our pickup for what reason, exactly?

When she jumped back in the passenger's seat an accomplished visage brightened her face. "Ok, let's go." I didn't ask any more questions just then for in truth, I didn't want to know. I snapped the radio on again, wrested the Bug Truck into first gear and we peeled out.

After school we stopped by our usual corner store and picked up the ritual after school pizza pocket and Dr. Pepper. I had a hard time eating, given the horror behind me that was separated from my snack by a mere pane of glass. I couldn't take it anymore.

"Boog," I pled, "why did you pick up that leg?"

"I'm gonna pull a joke on Dad," she said. A mischievous smile crossed her face. "But you have to swear to me no matter what, no matter how hard he grills you, you won't rat me out."

This posed a real conundrum. I needed more details before I could commit to a conspiracy. "What are you gonna do?"

"You'll see."

That night after we'd all gone to bed I heard a scream from the direction of Boog's room down the hall. I heard Dad scuffling around, trying to get out of bed and running into things, cursing. He was yelling, as is his tendency when alarmed. Anger is the automatic reaction before he learns what's going on. This trait historically tickled my sisters and me. We often joked about it behind his back.

I stayed in bed with the cover pulled up to my nose, eyes wide in the dark, just listening to the racket. Dad sounded a lot like Walter from The Big Lebowski.

"What in GOD'S name is THAT?!!" He sputtered, furious. I heard Boog feigning innocence. She was good at that.

In the preceding months Boog had become obsessed with The Godfather Trilogy. She quoted extensively from the first two films and mastered spot on imitations of nearly every character. She'd taken particular interest in the scene where The Don leaves the head of a prized horse in the bed of a Hollywood movie producer. So Boog waited that night until everyone went to bed. She sneaked outside, pulled the horse's leg out of the truck and planted it in her own bed. She placed a forged threatening letter nearby. It was written in block lettering. Then she slid back under the covers and screamed.

I heard Dad questioning Boog in his agitated state. "Who would do something like this?" He demanded. "Who would have the balls to come in my house with me in it and leave something like that? Only a psychopath!" I cringed in my bed, knowing full well I'd soon be pulled into the melee. My guess was correct. I heard loud stomping down the hall.

"FAITH! Get in here, NOW!"

I shuffled into the living room where the family gathered in their night clothes. Everyone was bleary-eyed, save for Boog, who now looked more nervous than mischievous and Dad, whose eyes held an apparent murderous intent.

"Do you know who did this?" He demanded of me as he waved the forged note in the air. I took the letter from him and looked it over. Boog had gone to great pains to manufacture an impressive threat letter. I pretended to pore over its contents while trying to decide if I should aid this sick joke or rat Boog out and perhaps prevent my father from suffering a massive heart attack. His face was an unnatural shade of red. His nostrils flared.

I was and am a notoriously horrible liar. My parents busted me every time I attempted a lie. I displayed all the classic signs. Glance off to the right, twiddle thumbs, fidget in seat, cheeks flushed and sweaty. All of it. I decided to pull a Bill Clinton that night and told a half-truth without filling in any pertinent details.

"Well, I didn't do it! I've been asleep since I went to bed!" I cried, to persuasive effect. Dad eyed me closely, and persuaded for the moment, moved on.

"I'll tell you one thing," he raged, "I'm going to find out who did this and when I do, they're gonna get a few Molotov cocktails tossed in their car! It's a dangerous person who'd do something like this. An animal! You better hope it isn't some prank your friends pulled. And tell your little

boyfriends when I find out who did it there will be

consequences." He delivered the last part with a low,

sobering tone.

Boog and I slunk back to our beds. I went to sleep

angry with my sister for not fessing up after she'd

successfully executed her prank. Mad at myself because I

knew if left to stew long enough and given enough

circumstantial evidence, Dad's potential to go ballistic was

real.

Next morning we got up to leave for school and Dad

was waiting for us on the couch. He hadn't been back to bed

apparently. In his hand I noted a pen and paper. It appeared

he'd been making notes. He didn't say much and we scuttled

out the door as quickly as possible. I chastised Boog for not telling the truth after we left.

"I got scared," she said, "I didn't know he'd freak out *that* bad."

"You put a horse leg in your bed. What exactly did you expect?"

We rode on in silence for the remainder of the drive. I made up my mind to tell Dad the truth when we got back home. It's a serious deal to rat out a sibling, but quite another to aid and abet a parent in the commission of a felony. When we walked in that evening we found Dad in the same spot on the couch again, waiting.

We sat down and he said, "I know you did it Boog."

I was surprised to see relief wash over her face. She'd been found out rather than forced to confess-always the easiest option. Dad's reaction amounted to another surprise. He wasn't upset at all.

"How'd you figure it out," she asked.

Dad held up the threat letter and some homework he'd dug up around the house. "Thing is, the next time you write a threatening letter, you need to make sure not to use distinctive markings in your writing. I probably wouldn't have been able to tell, it was pretty good block lettering, all except for your Capital G."

We leaned in and peered at the letter next to Boog's homework. Sure enough, on both documents we noted a distinct arrow shape on the inner mark that could not be mistaken. Dad laughed and congratulated Boog on the care she'd taken to execute her prank, and noted how stealthy she must have been to get that leg in the house undetected.

The only question he had was the most obvious.

"Where in the hell did you find a horse leg?"

"Dad, it's a long story," Boog said, and sauntered off down the hall. She walked into her bedroom where the sheets were freshly laundered. The room smelled of bleach, Boog's favorite cologne Obsession, and just the faintest soupçon of horse hair.

Rig Up Brit Strips

While I worked as an attorney in southern Oklahoma I met a pretty interesting fellow. He was very different from the country gents to whom I'd become accustomed. We were both young business professionals in the same community and met at a local radio station function. He was a natty dresser and spoke with a British accent. Let us call him 'Nigel', for our purposes here. Nigel spotted me sitting alone and pursued me from the start. The accent proved too much to resist for a girl who came from a rural Adair County family that laughed hysterically at British sitcoms and quoted Monty Python's Holy Grail in its entirety. Oh, the novelty.

We quickly became enamored with each other, he with my pancake syrup flavored lip gloss, and I with his traditional English breakfasts. I don't cook, so chefs have a particular draw in my case. I took the Brit back to meet my family in the hills of eastern Oklahoma. They were similarly charmed by the accent. Everyone, that is, except my sister. She said from the beginning he couldn't be trusted.

That weekend we went down to the creek that runs through the hollows on my grandfather's land. We wanted to take part in what Okies call "Skipping Rocks", an embarrassingly banal, but oft-employed competition of skimming rocks across the surface of the water and counting how many times it skips before sinking to the bottom. I was secretly amused and excited to see how my foreigner boyfriend might fare amongst the hillbillies, particularly since he'd referred to this practice as "Tossing Stones", a misnomer that elicited a great round of laughter from the family. They called him 'Fancy Pants' behind his back because he was quite proper in his speech and demeanor, especially compared to anything we'd ever encountered, save for on television. Nigel was what the men in my family referred to as a "Dandy". I also knew him to be gangly and uncoordinated. He regularly injured himself in my presence, so much so that I found it necessary to maintain an injury log.*

So, it came as a shock to us when The Brit picked up his first rock and zipped it right across the creek. It planed across the surface as if on wings, skipping at least 25 times before coming to rest on the opposite bank. This feat was unprecedented from a newcomer. He'd blown the rest of the family out of the water on his first try, after all our years of experience at "stone tossing".

Everyone stood out on the porch that evening, talking and watching the country summer sky. We had a menagerie of stray dogs that dragged themselves up from the highway. My parents have soft hearts and could never turn any of them away. But on occasion dog fights broke out, and so it happened on this night. My dad was recovering from back surgery and he was "stove up", as we say in the Oklahoma hills. He tried to break up the fight but the ruckus carried on for several minutes, a rolling ball of snarls and fur.

My mom grabbed a broom to try and wedge the dogs apart. The Brit stood there all the while, daintily smoking his cigarette and watching the melee in disdain. On our drive back that night, I chastised him for failing to help my dad. He was fairly shocked to learn I might expect him to be involved in such a mess.

On our next visit to see the family we found ourselves gathered on the porch at dusk once again. My father had taken up wine-making and became quite passionate about the little vineyard planted in the front half of his acreage. He'd strung up several strands of twelve gauge wire across the vineyard in an attempt to train the vines up properly.

That night another dog fight broke out. The dogs took out across the yard nipping and barking. The Brit looked over at me and, recalling my scorn from the previous incident, began to run across the lawn after the dogs to stop the fight and redeem his honor. We stood watching as he launched full-tilt in the waning twilight. None of us thought to sound the alarm as we didn't timely realize the inevitable. Without warning he sprinted neck-first into the vineyard wires. His feet flew straight up in cartoonish fashion.

The Brit sprawled on the ground, hands at his neck. I ran out to him, leaned over and cried, "Oh my God, Nigel, are you ok?" His eyelids fluttered and he looked up at me. He answered after a brief moment of silence, in his fine British accent.

"I cahn't breathe."

Afterward my Dad attached little neon swatches of material to the vineyard wires to ward off future foreigners from clotheslining themselves. To this day our family affectionately refers to them as "Brit Strips".

Exhibit A

Maintain Nigel's Injury Log

1. Tripped over own bag.

2. Hit head on exercise equipment.

3. Suffered leg cramp.

4. Burned hand on stove.

5. Toe bitten by dog.

6. Injured shoulder while retrieving frozen pizza.

7. Sat on own testicle.

8. Electrocution via phone charger.

9. Sat on other testicle.

10. Near decapitation via grapes.

Light Up a Can of Corn On the Union Jack

My relationship with The Brit began to flag and I realized with certainty we would never make it long term. I told him as much and tried to break things off, but he became extremely agitated and threatened suicide. He drove out to my house and acted as though he would hang himself from the pecan tree in my front yard. My sister Missy and her boyfriend were visiting again, and Philip went out to stop Nigel from going through with the act.

I should note here that Philip is a former UFC fighter and a national champion wrestler. When he went out to stop The Brit from hanging himself, they began to struggle with one another. Imagine a rather thin and proper English guy wrestling a UFC fighter. Realizing that Philip would overpower him, the Brit began to bite his fingers. Philip felt sorry and looked back at us for direction as they struggled. He clearly didn't want to hurt Nigel, as he was already in a poor state. Philip lifted The Brit out of his shoestring noose. Nigel jumped in his SUV and sped away, spraying the three of us with gravel from the driveway. I hoped that would be the end of my British Era, but one more disastrous chapter, and the most dramatic one, had yet to play out.

During that time I was working on my first novel, Ezekiel's Wheels. I wrote mostly on the weekends home alone, usually with a glass of wine. It was late on a Saturday evening and I was well into my third chapter, as well as a third glass of vino, when my front door flew open. It was The Brit and he was livid.

I didn't feel frightened for my own safety at all. I just needed him to leave. I demanded that he get out but he refused to go, at which time I should have called the police. But I lived in a home that was located on the property where I worked, and I feared a big dramatic scene. He swore that the only way he would leave would be if I agreed to drive him home. I had a sinking feeling in the pit of my stomach as I walked to the back to fetch my purse and keys. My conscience tried to warn me.

When I walked back out Nigel was on his cell phone. Upon seeing me he ended the call and hurriedly shoved the phone in his pocket. An overwhelming sense of danger came over me. I felt that something was about to go very wrong. Every impulse in my body said, "Do not get in that vehicle." But I pushed all those intuitions back down inside.

Nigel got in the passenger's seat and I behind the wheel. We started driving the seven miles toward his loft. His behavior was alarming. He acted very nervous and kept looking in the side view mirror. I took care to drive perfectly, five miles per hour below the speed limit with careful use of turn signals. Something told me to turn off and take the back road that bypassed the town. I turned on my signal and he barked, "What are you doing?! This isn't the right way!" Just as the words passed his lips and I began to turn, the twirling blue and white lights blazed in the night sky behind me. I felt in an instant the devastation and guilt of the horrible series of choices I'd made.

As soon as the patrolman walked up to the window I volunteered the truth. "I've been drinking. I've had several glasses of wine tonight." He appeared to be shocked by my honesty and then asked me to step out of the vehicle. He took me out of earshot of Nigel and I said, "I already know why you stopped me, officer. You got a report called in, right?" He paused for a moment and then nodded confirmation.

I told the officer everything about the night's events leading up to that point. The officer gave me a field sobriety test and I passed. He was inclined to let me go until he went back to the Jeep and found a cup of wine I'd brought along for the drive. The bottom line was, regardless of circumstances, I'd broken the law and I had to go to jail. He knew I'd been truthful and I overheard him giving a very stern speech to Nigel, though I'll never know exactly what he said.

Jail was much more about humiliation for me than imprisonment. I never paraded around naked in front of anyone, so it was with much horror that I had to strip off completely while a female officer observed me showering. Then she handed me a one-piece zippered orange jumpsuit. Given my body type, I've always chosen a wardrobe designed to flatter my height, often choosing shorter skirts to emphasize my legs. This get-up showed off my legs, alright. It made them look like two toothpicks stuck in an orange. I looked just like a fruit cocktail at a misdemeanor reception.

They took me back and tossed me in the slammer. I lay back on a cement block and stared at the layers of paint covering the walls. Previous inmates apparently made a habit of scratching the paint off out of boredom or angst. It looked like twenty layers of paint covered those walls. Faded pastel blue paint. Someone who'd previously been in the very same cell before had scratched a message into the paint. It read, "Fuck The Boss Hog." That stuck with me for a long time. I still have an imagined image of the girl who memorialized her lonesome grief on that cell wall. Although in my situation I couldn't blame the Boss Hog. In any case I felt her despair.

I felt a sense that time had stopped altogether. Time, the precious gift we take for granted every day, became a limitless commodity in that cell. My market was suddenly flooded with time. I wished for an end to time. In that caged, painted box a single minute transformed into an hour. I couldn't possibly sleep. My mind revolted against me. It felt like a circus sideshow over which I had no control. The entire experience was surreal, as if I watched the whole thing from up above. I'm no psychiatrist but in casual laymen's terms I think part of my psyche must have detached and observed the action from afar, in order to ensure I didn't lose my mind.

Time stretched on and every once in a while I'd hear a shout but mostly it was just an awful, echoing silence, with nothing to distract me from contemplating the terrible decisions I'd made to ensure my arrival in just this place. I was only in for six hours, but it felt like six months. A guard came to the door and said I'd been bailed out. I blinked at her in disbelief. As we walked up front to get processed out and pick up my things, I realized there was no possibility my family could have known what had transpired. Even if they had known, they couldn't have traveled the distance to reach me in six hours.

"Who bailed me out?" I inquired. So far as I knew, only one person knew enough to bail me out, and that was the one who'd seen fit to help put me there. I told the guard, "Please, you don't understand. If I walk out of here and the person who posted bail is the same one who set me up, I'll be right back in here again for assault and battery." The guard remained stoic and unphased. Apparently I was not the first to ask to remain imprisoned after bail had been posted.

"We can't keep you in here, ma'am."

I stopped by a little window, where they shoved my belongings out in a little gray plastic tub. I gathered them up in my arms and looked over at a side room. Inside I saw a television monitor that displayed the precise area where I'd been made to disrobe. Several male police officers sat gathered around. By that time I was beyond humiliation and said nothing. I signed whatever I had to sign, took a deep breath and walked toward the exit.

When I reached the heavy brown double doors I felt as though my arms hadn't the strength to push them open. I turned my back and pushed them open with my backside. I left prison just like a crawdad. Ass first. The doors clanked shut as I turned to face what I already knew was there. The Brit stood there, somber, smoking a cigarette. He'd seen fit to put me in and then saw fit to get me out.

"I know what you did," I seethed, "the officer told me you called in a false report."

I was unable to look at him for fear I'd fly into a violent rage. He feigned innocence and denied my accusation. Swore on his life. But I knew, and he knew I knew. I tried to make the seven mile walk back to my house on foot, but a girlfriend intercepted me and gave me a ride.

When I finally made it home I collapsed on my couch and wailed. My dogs Franc and Beans tried their best to provide comfort. Beans licked my face while Franc sat nearby and howled at the ceiling. They shared my grief with me that night. Thank God they were there to love me. In that moment their love was the only confirmation that I was not alone. When the sun came up I called my mom. She said Nigel had called in the middle of the night to say I'd been picked up for DUI (but left out all other detail). He assured her that he would take care of me, they needn't come help.

I will never be sorry for telling the arresting officer the truth because he reflected the entire account in his police report. Plus, Nigel called the Highway Patrol the next day to file a complaint against the arresting officer who confirmed for me that a false report had been called in. The Hi-Po didn't take kindly to that. These combined factors directly resulted in the District Attorney dropping the charges against me to Reckless Driving. It is a humiliation to have that on my record but I know it could have been so much worse.

After my family learned the details of that night Missy became incensed. She called to announce her plan to eat a can of corn, poop on the Union Jack flag, and light the whole thing on fire atop The Brit's SUV. Somehow I convinced her that those six hours I spent in the clinck amounted to enough time for the entire lot of us, for all the rest of our lives. She finally relented and with that, it was time to move on. Thus concluded my British Phase.

Hear Iris and Teresa

Music speaks to me. Like most people I'm emotionally moved by music. It feels like spiritual worship to me, like the high I imagine some receive from attending church. The feeling is real and it is powerful. I have to limit my exposure to some artists, like Pink Floyd, because while a song can make me feel closer to The Creator, it also has the power to send me down a serious emotional spiral into depression. I'm pretty familiar with the triggers by now, so when the first notes of 'Is There Anybody In There' float out of the speakers, I make a desperate dash to turn it off before I hear any of the words.

But this is where I sound like a real moon bat. I've come to accept that important, timely messages and prompts to act come to me through songs. These moments have occurred here and there, but with regularity, throughout my life. One of the most extreme examples relates to the song *Iris* by The Goo Goo Dolls.

My son's Aunt Teresa helped him through a trying emotional time after his father and I divorced. They became extremely close. She bought him a bunny rabbit named H.R. and they cared for it together. She spent many hours comforting him and helping him feel loved and secure.

Teresa and her husband spent the weekend attending the celebrated rivalry between OU and the University of Texas football teams in Dallas. They headed north on I-35 toward Oklahoma City after the game. She rode in the passenger seat. A man who'd previously received numerous reckless driving tickets attempted to pass them on the left at an extremely high speed. When he clipped their bumper the vehicle flipped several times across the median. The extraordinary force caused Teresa to be ejected from the vehicle, even though she wore a seatbelt. When the flipping car came to a stop it pinned her beneath the car. In an extraordinary feat of devotion, Teresa's husband lifted the car off of her, but she was hurt too bad. There was nothing else he could do but comfort her as she faded away there by the darkened interstate. One of her favorite songs was *Iris* by The Goo Goo Dolls. *Iris* played at her funeral and from then on the song was imprinted in my mind.

Several years later I faced a crucial decision. My son's father and I were respectful and civil, but a discussion arose that perhaps our son would have a better, more stable life with his dad. I struggled day and night with the decision. The thought of not having my son with me was repugnant. In the deepest fiber of my being I did not want to let him go. But the fact remained that his father was much better off financially and could give him a life that, as a single mom, I just couldn't provide. I worked hard to be great at both parenting and my profession. Still, that meant he was left alone for a couple of hours every day after school. I needed to be sure I didn't make him stay with me for selfish reasons.

The internal conflict raged on until the day came when I was to drive to Oklahoma City to meet with his father and come to an amicable agreement on which of us would have primary custody. We both agreed we would not go through the courts. A contentious court battle was out of the question. We decided to put our son before ourselves, and for that I am eternally grateful for my son's father.

The previous day had been very emotional but on our meeting day I steeled myself. I flipped on the radio to ease my frazzled mind as I drove north. When I entered the city limits the first few notes of *Iris* began to play on the radio and a spike of intense pain associated with Teresa shot through my heart. I reached out and hit the scan button, desperate to make it stop. The radio flipped through the dials and to my shock it stopped on a different station where *Iris* continued to play. I sat dumbfounded for a moment. Incredulous. I had a little talk with myself.

"This isn't something supernatural, it's just a coincidence. Let it go."

So I reached out and hit scan one last time, convincing myself as best I could not to read anything into the timing.

I watched the green digital numbers flip through until they landed on a third Oklahoma City radio station. There, again, Johnny Rzeznik sang, *"You're the closest to heaven that I'll ever be And I don't wanna go home right now"*.

I relented. When I refused to accept a clear message, the messenger would not be denied. I had to be picked up, smacked around and put in my place. I believe it was the admonition I had to hear to be at peace that my son and I needed each other. He would stay with me. I walked in to meet his father without any lingering doubt. No more questions as to my ability as a mother or my intentions toward the relationship with my son. I also accepted a clear understanding that I might be the recipient of important messages from time to time, so long as I allowed myself to be open.

Fall For A Chicken Man

It's a pretty funny story, the way things started out. My grandmother was recovering from breast cancer and a mastectomy. I drove her to Tulsa for all her appointments throughout the process and on this day she had a post-op checkup. Everything looked great, she was a survivor. On the way home we decided to celebrate with a nice meal and a spin of some penny reels at the nearby casino.

I sat down at a machine called the Old Prospector. I didn't have much money at all so I was really just intent on biding my time. Out of the corner of my eye I saw a man stride past as though he had urgent business. It was the speed and determination of his gait that caught my eye. He turned his head slightly and caught sight of me. He did a double take. He walked over in a markedly different manner and stuck a hundred dollar bill in the machine directly next to mine. I discreetly took note of all this action and acted as though I hadn't noticed his presence. I did not want to be bothered, I did not desire small talk, and the last thing I wanted was a come-on from a stranger in a casino. I thought, "Oh *good*, here we go again." My experiences with interested men in those kinds of places were historically undesirable. I waited on the corny first line.

But he was charming instead. He started out by asking an intelligent line of questions, rather refreshing from the norm. His voice was startlingly deep with a strong country accent. Despite the accent I immediately knew he was smart. More than anything he struck me as very masculine. Not at all a traditional hunk and not a man most would consider very good looking, but the confidence and aggressive mannerisms made for a potent elixir. It isn't often I find myself immediately attracted to the opposite sex, but when I do I always turn awkward and lose my cool.

I began to stammer. I told him I had to go after just a few minutes of conversation and got up in a rush. When I started to walk away he laughed and said, "you might want your money?" In my rattled state I failed to realize I'd won nearly a hundred dollars on my machine. He handed the ticket over and ordered me a glass of red wine. I kept finding reasons to walk away from him but I was keenly aware that every place I went he was watching. Before he left that night I'd given him my phone number and agreed to meet for dinner in a week. I'd hardly left the parking lot before he sent the first text message. Over the next week we exchanged hundreds of messages and though I genuinely did not want to, I became enamored.

We arranged for our first date the following Thursday. During the week he inquired about my favorite wine. I told him my very favorite was a Pinot Noir from Failla in Napa Valley. I explained that it wasn't available in Oklahoma, but that I'd be flattered by any Pinot he chose. I went out and bought a fancy little black dress. My family went on and on about my appearance when I got all dressed up and I was so embarrassed. I felt a lot like that stupid Reba song. You know the one.

The moment I arrived he was waiting with a basket stocked with two bottles of Failla, chocolates, artisan cheese, some kind of fancy crackers and strawberries. The planning and effort overwhelmed me a bit because no one had ever gone to comparable lengths to romance me. Smitten is a fair word to describe my state that evening.

But I had to ask one question that kept plaguing my mind and I just couldn't shake it. It was essentially the last reservation I used to hold my budding emotions in reserve and I just couldn't keep it in any longer. As we prepared to leave for dinner I blurted out, "You aren't married, are you?" I studied his face carefully for any sign of deception. He looked me square in the eye, never blinked, and replied, "No, I'm not. I'm a single dad." I immediately began apologizing for myself.

`   "I'm so sorry, I'm really sorry to ruin this," I said, glancing at the floor. "You'd be surprised how many times…" I trailed off.

"No, I wouldn't be surprised," he replied, "you're a beautiful, smart, accomplished woman. I can only guess how many people want to be with you, married or not. But it's ok, because I am not."

He squeezed my hand and touched the side of my face. I took a deep breath and let go of the last fail safe I'd put in place to protect my heart.

For two weeks the Chicken Man pursued me and though I pride myself on my independence, I started to fall in love. I didn't want to. Romantic love has only ever been a great impediment for me. Most people need partners to get through this life and together they make a team that makes both individuals stronger and better. But it doesn't work that way in my case. Love makes me weaker, less productive, less creative and less fulfilled. But who can deny that intense feeling you get when you first start to fall for someone? Gets me every time. It's my kryptonite.

The Chicken Man was intense. He complimented everything about me. He was kind of a fanatic. When I tried to slow things down he would not relent. I said I could see him once a week but that wasn't enough. He wanted more. He stayed in constant contact, texting throughout the day while he was at work and calling every night. One evening I sat outside talking to him on the phone and for some reason I said, "I know things are moving too fast but I don't know, there's just something about you I trust."

There was just a moment of pause in return on the other end. Then he began to ramble on about something else. One thing the Chicken Man never ran short on was words. I heard all the truth I needed in that two second pause. I knew he'd just told me without saying a word that he was not a person to be trusted. As soon as we hung up I got online and did a cursory search of Oklahoma court dockets. That's when I discovered that the Chicken Man had been married twice already and was currently in lucky marriage number three.

I didn't call him back. I simply sent a text: "Chicken Man, are you married?"

No reply. I waited twenty minutes until I sent the next message.

"Chicken Man?" I needed to hear the answer from him.

The reply finally came in, "I am awaiting final divorce" followed directly by a message that read, "I will respect your wishes and not contact you again."

I replied to say, "I forgive you. Never contact me again. But take my advice, perhaps if you romanced your wife like you did me the past month, you might not find yourself going through a divorce right now."

I put my phone down and hung my head. The high I'd been floating on for the past month became the lowest low. Still, we hadn't been together that long. I'd call it a short, intense heartbreak made worse by the humiliation of being lied to and anger with myself for being stupid. But I knew I'd be ok.

My best friend took me for a weekend trip to Reno a few weeks after it was over to lift my spirits. I was already feeling much better and very grateful I'd found out the skinny on the Chicken Man when I did.

I got a message from my mom while I was gone. It read, "Dad's had a medical emergency. Come home as soon as you can." Upon arrival I heard the details that my dad had collapsed in the bedroom floor and was unable to walk. The doctors said he likely wouldn't walk again, but they scheduled a surgery in hopes they might reverse the damage.

When I drove to Tulsa to visit Dad I pulled in the parking garage and there was the Chicken Man, holding a basketful of assorted snacks for my family while they waited in the hospital. He handed me a tiny wooden treasure chest filled with silver trinkets and explained what each one represented. One simply read, "Faith", one was a paper airplane representing his passion for flight and one was a little pea pod with two beans in it. He said it meant we were two peas in a pod. He asked if, after my visit with Dad, I'd go to dinner and just hear him out. Like a moron, I agreed. I went up and spent two hours in the hospital room until the visiting schedule concluded. Dad was on heavy I.V. pain medication and went in and out of consciousness. At one point he muttered, "Does your boyfriend know karate?" I assured him that I did not have a boyfriend. We prayed together as a family.

When I walked out the Chicken Man was still waiting. He drove us to an Italian restaurant where he explained he'd been in the process of a divorce when we met and that he'd been separated and living apart from his wife for several months prior to our meeting. He explained that he'd been too afraid to come clean after we started dating for fear he'd never see me again. Like a moron, I believed him again.

I could list so many lame excuses on why I agreed to see The Chicken Man after that, but it doesn't matter. I made the wrong decision. I used to watch Dateline episodes and always wanted to reach through the screen and grab the poor women who got duped by sleazy money-grubbing cads. I wanted to shake them and say, "WAKE UP, LADY!" But I was worse than those ladies. At least they had some money to steal in the first place.

I told the Chicken Man, "If you ever lie to me again, about anything, for any reason, you'll never see me again."

Tears rolled down his cheeks and he said, "I promise I'll never hurt you again."

Incidentally, have you ever heard the Neil Young song, *'Stupid Girl'*, off the Zuma album? It's pretty killer, man. You should check it out.

Forgive the Big Kid

I've always been a big girl, from the time I was little. Always the tallest in class, boy or girl, always with a little extra jiggly padding my bones. My parents told my sisters and me from the beginning, as early as I could comprehend and maybe before, that we were beautiful, smart, and capable of accomplishing anything. So for the first part of my childhood I had no reason to question that admonition. I believed everything my parents told me and their bolstering of my self-esteem was no exception. I felt great confidence and though I was considerably bigger than every other girl in my school I took great pride in my appearance. I loved to wear pretty dresses and the bouncy curls from the squishy pink rollers my mom put in my hair at night.

But then in the fifth grade something happened that most adults would dismiss as silly. Nevertheless it became a turning point in my self-esteem. We were on the bus to a skating rink that night and for some odd reason a few older kids boarded. One of them was fifteen or so and I admired him. He was tall and skinny with long, shaggy hair. His face was marked with acne but I didn't care. He was a Big Kid and that made him a real rock star. Pretty punk and cool.

I'd chosen a seat toward the back of the bus and as drove I stared out the window, daydreaming about swirling lights on an illuminated rink. My skating skills were pretty junker, I couldn't skate backwards or turn circles, but I fantasized that maybe the Big Kid would ask me to Couple's Skate (oh, the romance).

I noticed when the Big Kid stood and slowly made his way toward the back. He stopped at every seat momentarily and spoke a few words to each girl he encountered. I snapped out of my day-dream and listened intently to pick up on what he might be saying. I soon realized he was systematically moving through and evaluating each girl on her physical appearance by saying, "Pretty" or "Not pretty". My sister Boog sat a couple seats ahead of me and I became quite anxious for her as he approached. I knew if he hurt her feelings I would have to take up for her, whether it was the Big Kid, a punk rocker or the finest dude in the world. I prepared myself to do so. But then I felt immense relief when he looked down at her and said, "Pretty". I wasn't at all worried for myself because I'd taken great care to see that my hair was curled that day. I'd even sneaked some mascara out of my mom's purse and my eyes looked great. My nails were painted a deep shiny pink color. I was beautiful.

The Big Kid stopped at the seat in front of me where my friend Patty sat. Patty was a bigger girl, like me, and rather shy. I felt scared for her. He looked down and said, "Not pretty". I watched Patty's head drop in despair. She looked gut-shot and devastated.

Then the Big Kid came to me. I raised my head up high and proud and met his eye with confidence. I felt no fear. He took one look at me, puckered his mouth in disgust and shouted, "Oh GROSS, NOT PRETTY!"

The pain was immediate and eviscerating. It took one guy less than five seconds to upend all those years my family spent methodically building me up. As an adult now I wish I could go back there to that little girl and put my arms around her. I wish I could tell her, "you're going to grow up to be beautiful in ways that mean so much more than the way you look". But I can't. That was over thirty years ago and it still lives in my psyche as though it happened just last night. That is why you will never hear me say anything but positive remarks to girls, or women for that matter. You never know the impact your words have on other human beings. I just bet if that Big Kid had really known the destruction and power in what he'd say he would never have said it.

I heard many years later that the Big Kid was killed in a tragedy. Shot down in a drug deal gone wrong. I didn't feel any sense of justice or victory. Just sorrow for the pain he must have lived with in his life. Now, as a Big Kid in my own right, I can understand that on that night he was carrying around some terrible pain and had to transfer some of it to me for some reason. It was too much for him to carry on his own. I just wish he was still around so I could tell him that, as it turned out, I was "Pretty" enough to help him carry it for a while.

Find A Worst Best Friend

It is a fairly common occurrence for married people to get divorced during their first year of law school. The Dean told us that interesting little tidbit during initiation. So that is just what I did. I left my marriage of four years and moved into a dinky apartment complex located catty-corner to the law school. I was depressed. My life had not gone according to plan. I'd lost my little family, my focus and my faith. I was destitute. When times like these descend from time to time I isolate myself. Pity is one emotion I cannot abide. I can't tolerate the notion that people perceive me as anything but strong and capable.

Across the grassy knoll lived another girl from my law school section called Christa. She was known (based on interaction with other students and professors) to be loud, conservative, opinionated and brilliant. She Am-Jur'ed most of our courses, which is to say she scored the highest grade on our final exams. Only one other guy rivalled her intelligence, and he was the son of an attorney who came from Columbia University. I regarded this woman with a wary eye. She was argumentative and brash, rather insensitive at times. When I moved into the apartment complex I hoped she would not experience any neighborly inclinations toward me. I held a little housewarming party in my new digs and invited a few classmates over. I did not invite Christa. But about an hour into the festivities I heard a persistent knocking on the sliding glass door. Christa stood there looking in on the reverie, a self-invitee. I let her in.

After that night she started coming over uninvited every day. Christa reminded me of Kramer from Seinfeld in some ways. She never knocked. Just slid right on in, took the remote control and changed whatever show I'd been watching. She was bossy on an intolerable level and had an unpredictable temper. She easily shrugged off the things I expected to make her furious, and blew her lid here and there on matters I never could've guessed might set her off. Oftentimes I found her to be quite rude with an unapologetic lack of a filter. She possessed an offensive level of brutal honesty and a disregard for the rules of civility and politeness valued by most people I knew. She also displayed a kind of fanatic insistence on our friendship and a rare loyalty that eventually broke down my walls. My horror and avoidance slowly began to switch to an endearing admiration.

We started frequenting a local college bar called O'Connell's on our breaks from class, where we played trivia games on a bulky electronic bar-top machine we called The Black Box. I'm still not sure how I earned a law degree over that period of time. I certainly earned a doctorate in that Black Box. Christa began dating a classmate and fell for him pretty hard, though she knew he wasn't serious about her. He was well-known to be charming and kind, and a player. He took her over to his apartment one evening and right in the middle of their make out session another girl from law school popped out of his closet in Glenn Close/Fatal Attraction style. She started punching Christa in the back of the head as she headed for the exit. Christa might talk a big game, but she's never interested in the actual exchange of physical violence.

One of the dishwashers at O'Connell's looked like a lot of trouble. His arms were covered in tattoo sleeves, his face was marked with scars and he wore his hat backwards. He carried himself with a bold swagger and often stared at me from around the corner on his breaks. I knew without a doubt he was a bad guy to be avoided at all cost. So I invited him over to my house. That night the dishwasher stole my car and took it for a joy ride. The next morning he showed up on my doorstep to explain that he'd wrecked it. I hadn't even realized my car was gone, I just assumed he'd left on foot. I collapsed into a teary pathetic heap, unable to speak and completely at a loss. I had no resources to get my car back, no family nearby to call for help.

Christa walked in the apartment (again, no knock),

and demanded to know what was happening. When she discovered the details she threatened the dishwasher with his life. This little 5'4" woman got up in this guy's scary, scarred-up grill and dressed him down. He was taken aback. Clearly people never spoke to him like that. He said, "I don't think you understand who I am or what I'm capable of." But Christa never blinked once and through my tears I noted a glint of fear in his eyes. She took him by the arm and physically threw him out of my apartment.

After that day, although I remained embarrassed whenever Christa said something rude or talked too loud on her cell phone in restaurants, I no longer cared that she didn't follow the rules of civil society. She was on my side and she was loyal. Everyone could use a sidekick like that.

She drove an old Jeep and I figured she was poor like

me. Never one to dress in designer clothes or carry expensive bags like many others in law school, Christa stuck mostly to jeans and sweatshirts. Then she invited me to a fundraiser in her hometown a couple of hours away and we were supposed to stay in her parents' home. When we rolled up I thought a massive spaceship had descended and landed in the field of a country club neighborhood. The home was massive by any standards, but by my own Adair County experience the place was a mind-blower. I thought it looked like some kind of crazy resort rather than a home.

Later that night I said, "my God, you never said you were RICH." But in typical Christa style she shrugged it off and acted like it wasn't worth mentioning. She continued to regard wealth with that same casual demeanor throughout our relationship, even after she made her first few million dollars. I think that's an important factor on how our friendship endured all these years. She's my Worst Best Friend [hereinafter, "WBF"].

After law school WBF hired me to work as in-house counsel for her family's manufacturing company. We worked there for about six years before they sold the company and I left to move back home and finish up my first novel. WBF moved to Dallas. Every few months or so she'd call me up to schedule a vacation. I could never afford to go on these trips myself, but she never complained about that and we took several grand adventures together. The first of these happened in the Dutch Antilles. She booked us into an all-inclusive resort. The island is situated at the southernmost point of the Antilles. My family was concerned about the potential for hurricanes. I'd done my research and informed them that their fears were unfounded. Hurricanes never struck this little island because it was too far south.

The tropical storm struck the island on our second night there. I watched out my hotel window as sheets of rain came down and palm trees bent horizontal in the gale-force wind. Nothing could be done but to go down and have a glass of wine in the resort bar. But when I arrived all the people were scurrying about in a panic and packing things up. As an Okie well-accustomed to raging floods, searing drought and deadly tornadoes, I conducted myself like a typical rude American. I demanded to know why everyone was freaking out over a little bit of rain. No one seemed concerned with addressing my inquiry. I gave up at last and went back up to bed. When I awakened next morning I discovered the island had been hit by one of the worst storms in its history. The storm swept up and killed some of the islanders. This was the beginning of my education on sensitivity to other cultures.

When the locals start freaking out, it's a pretty good sign to pay attention.

The next voyage took us to Jamaica, the Caymans and Cozumel. WBF always had a dream that the two of us would one day audition for the Amazing Race. I'd never watched the show but she was convinced our individual characteristics would complement one another to make the greatest pair in the show's history. She's brilliant with numbers and reason, very detail-oriented and I ... well, I guess I'm creative and instinct-driven. She decided to sign us up for a simulation of the Amazing Race on Cozumel. Problem was, we were due to start at 8a.m. and I dragged back to the room at 5 a.m. after a long night of rambling. I collapsed in the bed drooling and snoring. Her alarm went off and by some miracle it woke me up. My mind was foggy with cobwebs. I rolled onto my elbow, propped myself up and opened one eye.

"Why aren't you getting up?" I asked.

"We're still gonna do the race?" She perked up immediately.

"NO!" I thought to myself, but I got up and dragged my carcass to the shower. I mentally prepared myself for a miserable day.

The Amazing Race was a combination of clues, riddles, mazes and physical challenges spread out over the cramped streets and alleyways of a little tourist city on the ocean. I sized up our competition as we prepared to get started. Our competitor-couples were mostly married pairs: a couple from England, a German guy and his wife, a determined-looking Japanese family. I had assumed the other contestants would share my apathy for the competition but I noted they were all quite studious, poring over maps and materials we'd been given. I was so annoyed. Then I looked over at WBF and saw that she too studiously leafed through the documents, a determined look on her face.

Our first stop was a museum. We were supposed to use clues to find a certain sculpture and then use the title of that sculpture to fill in words on our Amazing Race sheet. It was crowded and people were jostling each other about. I stood off to the side trying to keep from ralphing into an ancient vase when one of the contestants nudged me out of the way in order to read a placard. Things got personal. I still didn't believe we had a chance but I went over to WBF and said, "OK, let's go for the win."

We were in fourth place when we raced out of the

museum. Our next stop was a historical marker from which we had to decode a message. I'm good with words so I instantly solved the code. WBF wanted to work through the entire puzzle. "Do you want to win this?" I asked. She decided to trust me and we flew off to our next challenge, a short jaunt on a glass-bottom boat over a shipwreck. This posed my greatest challenge yet. I still felt like I might toss my cookies at any moment but I grabbed an Orange Fanta and guzzled it. I made it through the challenge burping soda the entire way. The crew shot looks of disgust at one another, but it was either belch or barf and I felt I'd chosen wisely.

After we got off the boat we had to run to the challenge I could not complete: miniature golf. I have a prejudice against golf, as we've already established here, and nothing offends my constitution so much as wielding a club.

A club in my hands means there's some imminent danger. So WBF allowed me to rest while she completed that entire challenge on her own. Obviously, she's a golfer, dude.

The race reached its completion at a little restaurant in a back alley where they brought out salty chips and ice cold margaritas. We sat and waited on our competition to arrive. We smoked the rest of those fools by at least fifteen minutes. We were wiped out when we got there, but after a few minutes with a cold drink we recovered nicely. When the other teams began to stagger in we were kicked back, cool and composed, with first place medals slung around our necks, just waiting. Our competitors made no attempt to mask their loathing. Together, WBF and I managed to unite the world there in that quaint Mexican city. But for a moment, Germans, Japanese, British, even other Americans all came together in united contempt for a couple of Okie tarts. We were happy to oblige.

Avoid Vegas

WBF decided we should make a road trip to Vegas. The plan was to drive straight through with WBF, myself and our good friend Jacelyn taking shifts. The only music we could all agree on was cheesy 80's pop. We loaded up on CDs stocked with bands like Frankie Goes to Hollywood, Flock of Seagulls, Duran Duran and Pet Shop Boys*. Nothing makes you drive hard and fast like the 80's. We figured our trip would take around fifteen hours, one way. We hadn't made it out of the Oklahoma panhandle before I became impatient. I asked to break our shift schedule and just drive as far as I could myself. I hate to ride. Both of the girls agreed. We'd fashioned a comfy little nest in the back of WBF's Jeep Cherokee for naps.

I enjoyed the sights along the way. Albuquerque in particular struck me as possibly the most beautiful city I'd ever driven past. When we drove through the Painted Desert tiny hard bits of snow pelted the windshield. The mysterious beauty of the west was not lost on me. We decided to swing by the Grand Canyon, just a couple of hours out of the way. I'd never been before and it seemed a real shame to pass it by on the way to a seedy joint like Vegas. WBF wasn't too excited about it but for once I had a partner there to overrule her opinion.

We parked, got out and walked a short distance to a designated public viewing spot. I immediately couldn't catch my breath. The vastness of it was more than my mind could encompass. The striations in the rock and their alternating bands of red, brown and gold reflected the sunlight. The darkness and shadow crept up the edges of the canyon as we looked for the bottom to that incomprehensible sight. The hawks, mere specks in the interior, caught rides on the drafts buffeting the interior, cruising with ease in that great wide wonder. Barely visible in the depths snaked the blue ribbon of the Colorado River. It was completely dwarfed. A massive force of energy itself, capable of powering entire cities, reduced to a mere thread. The smallness of my self was never more apparent. The realization left me with a feeling of enlightenment rather than fear. I didn't amount to even a speck of stardust glistening there on the edge of oblivion. Freedom felt raw and real there. I could go anyplace in the world from that spot and do anything, it didn't matter. I amounted to an inconsequential random gathering of elements. My soul swelled with these life-changing realizations when WBF said, "Yeah, I get it. It's a big hole in the ground. Now let's go to Vegas." She really is the Worst Best Friend in the history of the world.

I drove on and since I'd assumed chauffeur responsibilities both girls alternated taking catnaps. I was rolling on very little sleep and it began to wear on me. We were closing in on our destination and I was desperate to reach our room and get some sleep. The sight of Hoover Dam brought some relief, it signaled we hadn't far to go. We topped a mountain and then I saw it. The longest line of traffic of all time. I was incensed. We sat there and measured our progress by inches per hour. The entire line ground to a complete stop and we idled for over an hour. I rubbed my eyes and turned up the radio. The CD switched and Flock of Seagulls came on. The queer, static notes struck an odd impulse within. I turned the song up as loud as it would go, rolled the windows down and opened the car door.

"What are you doing??" WBF demanded.

I looked back and said, "I ran."

I hopped out from behind the wheel with the engine still idling and began to run alongside the stalled traffic. It was a spectacular up-close view of the dam, that alabaster-white behemoth. Off in the distance I could just make out the haze of Las Vegas. I ran until traffic began to crawl again. Perhaps it was the sight of a madwoman running in the rearview that helped the people decide to move. I ran back to the car and hopped back in behind the wheel.

"Now we're moving girls!" I shouted, winded but energized to make the final leg of the drive.

At long last we made it to The Strip. My inclination to sleep was completely gone, maybe because of that dam sprint, not to mention the neon, ziggity zag, flashy lights that never stopped calling my name. I hadn't brought much money for the trip. I was interning at an Oklahoma City law firm for $10 an hour so after bills I never had much left over at all. But I'd stuck back $200 for gambling money and food. Before I left my dad called and said in his oft-subversive way, "When you walk in the casino walk directly to the first roulette wheel you see and put it all on black."

I don't think he meant ALL OF IT, including my food money, but that's how I interpreted it and I always listen to my dad. So I walked right up to the roulette table and put it all on black. Every last penny. WBF stood by, shaking her head in disapproval. Jacelyn smiled, her eyebrows raised in great anticipation as the little ball rolled around and around, bounced a few times and landed right in its blessed little

black resting place.

I took my money in an overjoyed state, doubled in

just a matter of seconds. Double the money, double the fun, I

figured. We rolled our suitcases on up to our shared suite. I

was so jazzed about my big win I decided to demonstrate my

agility for the girls by executing a full somersault on the bed.

At the end of the room sat a massive oak armoire that

housed a big screen television. I made sure both my friends

were watching and got a couple of good bounces to build up

momentum. I executed proper somersaults all the time on

the trampoline back home and landed on my feet every time,

no sweat. I started with plenty of room, knowing I'd need a

little space for steps after I stuck the landing. But something

went wrong in my calculations. After I did a perfect flip in the

air my feet landed a bit behind my body and I found myself at an odd perpendicular angle. The trajectory shot me head long right into the armoire. I hit HARD and then crumpled in the floor. My friends did not hesitate; there was no pause of concern. They burst into violent hysterics. Jacelyn came over at last to see if I was bleeding.

"I might've died!" I protested their cruel reactions.

The rest of that evening amounted to one example after another of why I must be banned from that filthy den of iniquity. We hadn't left the room for more than a couple of hours before I'd lost all my money. I went to the ATM until the machine said I couldn't come back again for 24 hours. I didn't have a red cent to my name, not even for a cheap fast food burger. WBF told me I would just have to starve as she refused to enable my bad habits any further.

"I'm not hungry anyway," I sniffed. I was famished.

Jacelyn bought a meal deal that came with two burgers. She finished one and yawned. "Oh, I'm so full, there's no way I can finish this," she said and winked.

WBF rolled her eyes while I ate the charity burger. I wasn't too worried because I knew I had a half-eaten bag of Cheetos in my purse upstairs. I figured if rationed properly they'd last me until I could get back to Oklahoma.

***

Several years passed before WBF asked me to return to Vegas. This time we both had regular, well-paying professional jobs and hence, a little more money, which is a terrible reason to return. She'd found herself a man-feller, so she wasn't quite as boisterous as she'd been on our previous adventure. We went to dinner at some high-end gourmet joint and I perused the menu. I'm always up for something different and I spotted something I'd never seen before. This was a concoction I never knew existed in even my wildest dreams: Lobster Mashed Potatoes. I ordered it without hesitation absent any accompanying entrée. It was the only thing I needed to complete my life in that moment. Just a chance to pass a spoon of buttery comfort-laden potatoes filled with lobster – that's all I needed. That plus a glass of Chardonnay. I immediately sent a text to my sister back in Oklahoma: "After all this time I finally met my one true love. His name is Mr. Lobster Mashed Potatoes. We're due to be married soon."

After dinner my lame WBF went up to our suite to retire but I wasn't quite ready yet. I didn't care to gamble any more but an in-house concert was scheduled and I decided to attend. I sat alone, choosing to stay apart from the crowds. It didn't take long before I focused on the band's lead guitar player. The front man was ok, but he was no Diamond Dave. The whole band was good enough to warrant attention but the guitar player was stellar. I'd seen many impressive guitarists in my time but this guy was something extraordinary. I sat and looked on in awe without masking my admiration for his prodigious ability. I danced a little on my own and before long I noticed the guitar player was watching. He came down to my seat on their set break and we struck up a conversation about music. It's easy to assume a vapid exchange of sexually-charged flirtation. But that assumption is completely wrong. We talked about our favorite musicians and artistic influences. We shared an affinity for Bob and Neil. In just the short time we spoke he confided in me about his troubled childhood and how he was becoming alienated with the life of a musician. When it was time to return to his performance he asked me to stay until after the show.

The guitarist was really small. Petite, with long sleek black hair and almond-shaped eyes. Quite feminine in appearance, actually. I towered over him at 6'0", at least six inches taller. I'm sure I outweighed him by at least fifty pounds. Nonetheless, we shared a real intellectual and artistic magnetism. I waited for him and he played even better during the second set. Afterward he returned to talk again. During the discussion I was surprised when he leaned in and kissed me. It felt like a genuine act of affection. I gave him my number and headed back up to the room.

The next morning WBF woke me up at the crack of dawn to inquire what I'd done the night before. I was confused by her line of questioning. I told her I'd just stayed at the hotel and attended the concert. "Yeah right," she said. "I walked through the lobby last night and spotted you making out with some tiny Asian chick."

My little musician friend sent a message later that night to invite me out on The Strip. But I couldn't go. You see, I was already committed to leftover Mr. Lobster Mashed Potatoes, who waited for me with devotion in the refrigerator.

***

I might've predicted all the subsequent Vegas mishaps if I'd just learned a lesson from my first trip there. I was only nineteen and my beau proposed with a big diamond ring. I said yes. His mom immediately began talking to me about planning a proper wedding, something I'd never considered before. She sent little samples of gifts for the wedding party and ideas for floral arrangements. I made it through a week of these details before I decided I didn't want a proper wedding. I didn't care about doilies and lilies or the like. Not in the least. I aired my protests and together we decided we'd just take care of the whole thing in Vegas. Sounded simple.

His side of the family agreed, they loved Vegas. My family, or at least some crucial elements of my family, registered their protest. My grandfather sat me down over breakfast and took issue with my decision, something he rarely did. He explained that he understood my reticence with the tedium of planning a big hoopla, but he didn't want me to go to Vegas. "You can just go down to a little church here and say your vows," he explained, "that way your family can be there to see it. If you go to Vegas some of us won't be able to afford to go. But more importantly, you need to say your vows in a church." My grandfather was incredibly wise and a deeply spiritual man. I considered his advice carefully but I knew if I tried to have a small ceremony some of my friends would hear of it and before too long it would become a big to-do. I thanked my grandfather for his advice and booked the Vegas trip.

A few members of my family made the trip after all. My parents and sisters met us at the airport in Oklahoma City. My dad carried an antique green suitcase. It must have been fifty years old and one of the buckles broke off so the airline had to wrap tape around it to secure the contents for flight. I made note of his luggage compared to all the high end bags cycling around on the conveyor belt and I felt an odd sort of pride. It was a bit of a family trademark to be different. The hillbillies were headed for the big city lights.

Upon arrival in Vegas I went off with my parents and sisters. I was due to rendezvous with my Intended in our Luxor honeymoon suite. His fraternity brothers were in town for a big bachelor party. The morning of the wedding Boog and I went off on our own for brunch. We sat there without much to say, just staring down at our plates. David Bowie came on the overhead speakers and sang *'Modern Love'*.

"Never gonna fall for Modern Love/Walks beside me/Walks on by".

Boog looked up and blurted out, "Don't do it." She appeared to be surprised by her own words. I had to admit to a bad case of cold feet but I considered it to be typical pre-hitchin' jitters. I laughed at her and said, "I can't do that!

Everyone paid all this money to get here..." I trailed off. Boog

leaned in across the table and said in all seriousness,

"nobody'll care. Just get your things, we'll go get Mom and

Dad and fly home. Come on, let's go."

I thought about it. I'd announced to my entire family

at age ten that I never wanted to be married. I dreamt of

being a professional or some kind of leader, I wanted to

travel. Nothing in my makeup suited wifery very well. But in

the end, I couldn't run out on the wedding. So many people

had come who loved me. My family and the family of my

Intended had already spent so much money on the ceremony

and reception. We learned that a Vegas wedding can be just

as complicated and expensive as a wedding back home. And

then, of course, there was the fact that I really did love my

Intended, that's an important detail to add. Yes, I did love him. So Boog and I left our untouched eggs and went to prepare for the wedding. But that didn't stop me from creating a major disaster.

My dress was beautiful with a plunging neckline and a princess collar line. The train was nearly as long as I was tall. When I walked down the aisle my dopey baby sister was tasked with carrying the train. Boog was the Maid of Honor and she stood up front holding a red rose bouquet. I couldn't look at my parents in the pew because I knew I'd cry. As I walked down the aisle I felt a sharp tug that stopped me in my tracks. Missy was just eleven years old then and in her nervousness she stepped on my train. I looked back and saw that her face was a deep maroon color. Even at that age she was already stealing my thunder. I smiled to let her know everything was ok and we continued on.

After the deed was done we hopped in a limo and made our way to a place that would become my favorite restaurant in Vegas – the legendary Batista's Hole in the Wall. The ambiance of the place felt like a step back in time. It was dimly lit, with photographs of the Rat Pack and glamorous movie stars lining the walls. When we were seated a little old man came over to perform an Italian love song accompanied by his accordion. They served our party complimentary house red wine. Everyone laughed and took turns toasting the new bride and groom. Then it was time for little Missy to make her toast. My parents told me she'd been rehearsing her speech for some time so I prepared myself for sentimental words that would surely bring a tear to my eye. The room became quiet as she stood and cleared her throat.

"I'd like to say something for my sister Faith on her wedding night." Missy then proceeded to launch into a monologue of the family dinner scene from Eddie Murphy's The Nutty Professor.

"Can you wear a white wedding dress young lady? Sherman can wear a white tuxedo. Sherman never had relations. But I hope you have a strong back, because once you have had all of that man held up inside for 35 years you want it and want it and want it. WHEW! Might make your head blow off."

She'd no more uttered the first few words of her toast before my entire family began to laugh so hard we nearly lost our food. We knew the routine because Missy had been obsessed with that movie and watched it dozens of times. The other restaurant patrons were not so amused. They seemed to find Missy's performance in very poor taste. Perhaps Eddie Murphy was inappropriate for a wedding reception. As for me, some twenty years later, I've never heard a finer toast.

After dinner everyone splintered off in separate directions. My husband and I headed for the Luxor. My feet hurt and I was tired. We began to argue on the way back. For the life of me, I can't remember the reason, but I can definitively say it was my fault. By the time we reached the lobby the argument had escalated to a full tilt fight. My temper flared out of control and I pulled the big diamond off my finger and held it in front of his face.

"You wanna know what I think of this?" I reared back and tossed it. I mean I launched that sucker as far as I could. I can't help but imagine somewhere out there some dude who'd just gambled away his rent watched that ring fall out of the sky and looked heavenward to say a prayer of thanks.

When I tossed the ring my poor husband stood there in disbelief for a moment. Then he sprinted off across the casino floor dodging cocktail waitresses and slow-moving tourists. I took the opportunity to run away. I rode up the elevators to the honeymoon suite and locked myself in the bathroom. The husband followed me up after a few minutes. By some miracle he'd been able to retrieve the ring. He began to knock, asking me to come out and talk. But I refused and he eventually gave in. I thought he would just go on to bed but then I heard him talking on the phone. Then I heard him yell, "Faith, your mother's on the phone!" It was a dastardly trick. He knew I wouldn't leave my mom waiting on the phone. It was 1 a.m. and I knew she'd long been asleep. So I sheepishly unlocked the door and took the receiver. Ma went ahead and talked me down off the ledge. I hung up and went to bed. I never noticed the champagne and rose petals beside the heart shaped Jacuzzi tub until the next morning.

■■

Exhibit B

80s Road Trip Soundtrack

1. Every Breath You Take, The Police
2. I'll Wait, Van Halen
3. In Your Eyes, Peter Gabriel
4. The Promise, When In Rome
5. Head Over Heels, Tears for Fears
6. Land Down Under, Men At Work
7. I Ran, Flock of Seagulls
8. Dancing in the Dark, Bruce Springsteen
9. Take Me to the River, Talking Heads
10. Your Love, The Outfield
11. Someone Saved My Life Tonight, Elton John
12. Drive, R.E.M.
13. Into the Night, Benny Mardones
14. Buffalo Stance, Neneh Cherry
15. Kiss, Prince
16. Eyes Without A Face, Billy Idol
17. Putting On the Ritz, Taco
18. West End Girls, Pet Shop Boys

Follow Your Call (Malawi)

After my arrest I felt a deep sense of shame and remorse for the awful choices I'd made. I knew I had to take equal responsibility. If I'd ended things with The Brit in a healthy adult way rather than letting the drama build to its ultimate crescendo the resultant drama likely wouldn't have come about. I noticed everywhere I went in the time after that I heard the song *'The Cave'* by Mumford and Sons. It seemed to follow me around. The lyrics struck me as particularly relevant to my experiences: *"I'll know my name as it's called again."*

A man I worked with, Mike, asked me to start attending a Bible study. He knew I was not inclined to take part in classes or organized religion, for that matter. But he knew just how to reel me in. He asked for my help building a class up from the ground floor. He said I had the capability to reach many people and that we could build something that would make a big difference for people in the community. He was a leader in a nearby church and I held him in extremely high regard. A kind and humble person, non-judgmental and wise, I watched him consistently live out the Gospel on a daily basis, not necessarily by words but in the way he loved people. I enjoyed the lessons we studied each week. The verses felt specifically chosen as a personal message for guidance in my own circumstances. I didn't care much for the big hoopla of the main church service so I stuck to the smaller meetings.

I don't recall exactly how I found myself in the main service one Sunday after class; I think Mike must have specifically asked me to go. A fellow named Brother Johnny got up and gave a presentation on the work he and others were doing in Malawi. I watched with great interest as slide after slide moved past, revealing a striking but poverty-stricken country, with great mountains and vast stretches of red dirt. But the thing that really put the squeeze on me was the children's pictures. I'm not necessarily a huge fan of children as a general rule, excepting my own son. But these children, their eyes appeared so kind and honest; their little arms and legs poking out of rags. I thought to myself, "what an amazing thing these people are doing over there," and that was the extent of my consideration.

At the presentation's conclusion, Brother John said, "We'd like to ask every one of you to pray, so that if you feel called to Africa you will listen and be obedient to that call."

An immediate pain ran through my chest. I sat up straight and cleared my throat. My instant reaction was

steeped in complete refusal. The possibility that I would go to
Africa was beyond ludicrous. I had a twelve year old son who
needed me. I had a job. Plus, it was … AFRICA. Terrorists
were kidnapping people in Africa. I'd seen it on the news.
NOPE. I dismissed the feeling right away.

The next Sunday the same experience happened
again, only this time I felt a physical push that caused me to
rock forward a step from the place where I stood. I gathered
up my purse, notebook and Bible and walked right out of the
church service, absolutely convinced I would not go back. I
threw my things in the passenger's seat and started up the
ignition. *'The Cave'* was playing on the radio. I drove straight
to WBF's house where she was busy painting her walls a
beachy green color. I waited for her to say something since I
was visibly upset. But nothing. She continued on with the
task at hand. I sat there for ten minutes before I couldn't

stand it anymore and blurted out, "I think I'm being called to Africa!"

Since WBF is the stable, unemotional one in this friendship I eagerly awaited her answer. She always advised me against everything I ever proposed, a natural naysayer, usually on the basis that I couldn't afford it. I knew this time she would give me a long laundry list on how Africa was out of the question, and how irresponsible I was to even consider such a notion given my pathetic financial status, my single mom status and my employed status. All my statuses pointed to no.

She wore a kerchief in her hair and never stopped working the paint roller. But her brow furrowed a bit and out of her came the reply of my worst nightmares. "If God's calling you to Africa," she said, "you should probably go." I sat slack-jawed in disbelief. I couldn't believe my Worst Best Friend would let me down like that. It had to rank as one of the biggest jerk moves she ever pulled, and there were so many.

My lack of enthusiasm for the Malawi trip was rooted in deep insecurity. The basis for my reluctance came from the absolute conviction that I wasn't good enough. I drank too much, I'd gone through a divorce and afterward lined up a string of failed relationships. I enjoyed colorful language and told dirty jokes with the guys at work. The certainty existed in my mind that I shouldn't be telling anyone anything about what was wrong with them or what they should do with their lives.

The first time I met with the Malawi team my suspicions were confirmed. Everyone in the room seemed so proper, so well-versed. I felt messy and awkward. Out of place. The great majority of that feeling came from my own self-doubt. But after the meeting that day someone from the team approached me with a plastic baggie full of prescription pain pills. "Excuse me, did you drop these? They were under your chair," she said. My cheeks flushed and I stammered, "No, of course not! I don't take any pills, ever." The extreme reaction made me look like a liar, but I was hurt that anyone automatically assumed that the new weird girl had dropped her dope in class.

That exchange came very close to derailing the whole deal. But with counseling from my trusted advisor Mike, I was able to let it go. Mike warned that I should expect a great number of obstacles in my way as I prepared for Africa. They would seem insurmountable in the moment, he explained, but if I stayed true to my calling, I would emerge on the other side and the resultant blessings would be more than I could envision.

As always, Mike told the truth that day. The greatest obstacle to come would be the loss of my job. The company I worked for sold to a competitor and after major disagreements with the new company's policies and their treatment of employees in general, I made the decision to leave the company and the area altogether. I moved back to eastern Oklahoma near my family, where I began serious work on completing my first fiction novel, Ezekiel's Wheels.

Take A Three Hour Tour

Some of the worst choices I made happened in college. The head coach for the OU women's basketball team asked me to walk on and try out for their basketball program. I'd received an offer to play on scholarship at Northeastern State, but declined both options. Instead, I accepted an elite academic scholarship that included a monthly stipend from the Phillips Petroleum Company (no relation, obviously). P.P.C. required a 3.75 G.P.A. as a stipulation for maintaining the scholarship, a pretty lofty standard for the brightest of students. But an officer for the company met with me privately and explained that I was an exception in the class of distinguished scholars selected for the program. My scores weren't quite as high as all the other Poindexters in the group, he explained, quite sober. But the essay I'd written in my application had been so different from the other applicants that they decided to give the scholarship to me instead of many other smarter eggheads. Apparently I was the only nerd in 1996 with enough ovaries to tell an oil company they better get a plan together for alternative energy, and quick. I thanked the corporate officer for telling me I was the bozo of the scholars and promptly set about losing my scholarship. I skipped almost every class that semester. I only attended one class religiously and that was my Creative Writing course, where I hung out with my professor after class, smoking cigarettes and discussing great literature. He asked about my future plans. I said, "I dunno, I'm supposed to be studying petroleum engineering, but maybe I'll go to law school."

"Don't waste your time," he advised, "you're a writer. That's all you are." That sounded like the worst advice anyone ever gave me. I earned the highest grade available in that class. I flunked all the rest.

I did manage to meet a nice guy named Dean at a frat party that year. We dated for a while but eventually I broke it off. One night I sat alone in my dorm room, broke and hungry, when the phone rang. It was the frat guy. He wanted to know if he could bring a bacon cheeseburger and a chocolate malt from Braum's. I weighed my options and decided I would absolutely reconcile for a burger. When he came up to my room that night he proposed a weekend trip to Shreveport. I hadn't traveled much at that point in my life so I was totally in for a road trip. I didn't bother to let my parents know I was leaving the state for a road trip with a dude. That would not have worked out well at all.

Dean was pretty square, he didn't touch drugs, unlike some of his frat brothers and I really liked that about him. He had a sense of stability about him that I craved. Before we took out on the road trip his roommate caught me in a moment alone and handed me a little rectangular paper tab.

"Take this when you get down there. Trust me, it'll be fun," he said and winked.

I shoved the tab down in my purse and didn't say anything about it to Dean. We set off on our grand adventure. We blasted the stereo in his fancy car all the way to Shreveport. He let me pick the music which I always consider a romantic gesture.

Upon arrival I experienced sensory overload. No one had ever taken me to a casino before and I walked in completely wide-eyed. I had two hundred dollars to my life so I walked up to the blackjack table and plopped down a hundred on a single hand. I won, and when the dealer paid me my chips I just got up and walked off with a country rube grin on my face. I had no idea dealers should be tipped. The next time I returned to the table he and the other card players weren't nearly as friendly as the first time, for some odd reason. Over the next twenty-four hours I lost every penny. On the second evening Dean wanted to go back and gamble some more but I was done with the whole scene, including the one where I was broke.

He went on down to the casino and I plopped on the bed, satisfied to relax in the cold room laid back and flipping through the tube. I looked around the room and my eyes settled on my purse. I considered the little tab in there. Dean, I knew, would be gone for several hours so I decided I would try it out. I was certain I could withstand any effects it might have on me and be over it by the time we had to go to dinner. Even if it felt awful, I reasoned, I could handle it there by myself and be just fine. So I ate the tab and lounged back on the bed, waiting to see what might happen. After ten minutes or so I actually felt relief that there hadn't been any effects. Convinced the roommate had pulled a prank, I flipped through television channels, completely relaxed.

But then I noticed the heavy drapes began to ripple as if a strong wind blew through the room. We didn't have any windows open in the room I was certain. I studied this phenomenon for some time until I noticed something moving on the ceiling. When I looked up I saw giant iridescent snowflakes turning and merging into one another, creating new snowflakes out of their confluence. Snowflakes were making snowflake families on the ceiling. It was awe-inducing, beautiful and at the same instant disconcerting. I didn't know I might lose control of my faculties, or that I might gain some ability to see things that weren't there. I struggled with it and forced myself to go through a short breathing exercise so as not to freak out. The realization struck me that I couldn't take it back, there was no way to hasten whatever effects might be on the way. I knew the more anxious I became, the weirder things would become. I calmed down a bit and focused on the television.

In my awe at the snowflake families, I'd completely missed the fact that Gilligan's Island was on. Everything I saw on that show was dazzling. The palm trees, the water, the cap'n's hat. But then something astounding happened. Ginger, the tall red-headed movie star appeared on screen and my eyes bugged out of my head. I'd never in my life observed such an other-worldly, dazzling being. Seemed to me something that beautiful and spectacular didn't even belong on this earth. My extreme emotions caused me to believe I was in love with Ginger from Gilligan's Island. It felt like the deepest affection I'd ever experienced in my life, such that it was almost crushing my chest. I couldn't look away. Finally, to my great relief, the program ended and I was able to peel my eyes away from the screen.

I knew that Dean would soon return to pick me up for dinner and I needed to get this stuff to wear off and quick. I decided the Jacuzzi would be the best answer. I ran myself a giant bath. The bubbles ran over the side of the tub and into the floor. I hoped the warmth of a long soak would bring me back to the ground by the time Dean returned. I was desperate to just be a normal human again. I laid back and closed my eyes. Slowly, I felt myself regaining control of my faculties, though every time I opened my eyes the bubbles jumped and popped and sparkled. Still, nothing freaky appeared where it should not be and I was no longer in love with a 1960's sitcom star. All good signs.

I stepped out of the tub, toweled off and wrapped a fluffy robe around myself. I approached the vanity in order to moisturize my steamed up face. When I gazed in the mirror I caught sight of the most terrifying monster I'd ever witnessed in any horror flick. The monster was me. Except my eyes were gone. The only thing left in their place was a solid red blob. I didn't feel like smiling, I was sick with terror, but somehow the MonsterMe was smiling back in the mirror. It was an awful, false smile, full of derision. I'd become evil over the course of just three hours. I flipped out and ran to the bed and covered my face with the covers. Every ten minutes or so I'd creep back into the bathroom to see if my eyes had returned, but they hadn't.

When I heard Dean come back I didn't get up. I was

curled in the bed with my back to the door. I pretended to be asleep but he came over and touched my shoulder. I flinched.

"Wake up, let's go get some food," he said in a jolly voice. The poor guy had no idea he was in a room with an evil no-eyed devil woman. I kept my lids squeezed shut so he couldn't see my monster-eyes.

"I'm so sick I can't go out," I whispered. He mercifully didn't bother me further and went out on his own to get something to eat.

I never did go to sleep that night. The next morning I took my things out to the car and placed them in the trunk. My back was in excruciating pain like I'd never felt before. The good news? Sometime in the night I got my eyes back. I rode back to Oklahoma with Dean that day knowing full well hallucinogens would never again do for the likes of me.

Thank you kind sirs, I'll ask you to pass on by. For you see, I

once encountered a devil-woman and indeed, She was Me.

Flash Your Odd Mac Muffin

The wardrobe malfunctions began early. I got this

really great dress in the fifth grade for the first day of school.

I felt like a superstar and my seat was on the front row. I

always chose the front row. Another consistent decision

throughout my life is my choice of panty style. I like 'em real

big. Always at least a couple sizes too big, the purpose of

which, of course, is to aid in maximum coverage. I might

wear a revealing little dress but you can guarantee that

underneath, a massive pair of underpants can be found. You

might compare them to my equivalent of a security blanket.

That day in the fifth grade I was a little tardy entering the room after the bell sounded. That was ok by me, it gave the entire class a chance to be seated at their desks before I walked past in my new pretty dress. When I sauntered past I noticed that not just the kids in the class but my teacher, also, took particular notice while I made my way up front to the desk. I reached back to smooth the back of my dress before I sat down except ... the dress was gone. My hand came to rest on a rather clenched and exposed cheek, along with my giant granny panties, the very culprit responsible for swallowing up my dress.

Some twenty years later I was walking the streets of Seattle. Again, I wore a cool black dress that seemed pretty sexy, but with a huge pair of panties underneath. You know, for security purposes. The city was wondrous. A new beautiful sight waited around every corner. I breathed in the salty air and reveled in the mild, overcast weather. We walked downhill for a couple of miles until we came to the famous market on the waterfront. I noticed murmurs behind us everyplace we went but I couldn't be bothered, there was too much to take in all around. I bent over and smelled the beautiful flowers overflowing from buckets all around. I'd never before seen so many flowers in one place. We strolled on and by the time we neared our hotel I felt confident we'd negotiated nearly every city block. We passed a group of men gathered on a street corner listening to music and shooting dice. I heard laughter after we walked by and figured one of them made some crass joke. We did look good after all. I wrote it off as vacant basal nincompoop behavior. Just as we prepared to make the last street crossing I heard an urgent voice call out. A striking, wicked-looking young woman approached. She had a short haircut with buzz lines on the side. Gauges hung in her ears and she wore a ring in her nose. Her body was covered in tattoos. She appeared extraordinarily cool and I wondered what she could possibly want with someone like me. She had a serious look that sullied her otherwise beautiful face.

"Ah, dude, your dress is tucked in your underwear. It's BAD," she said under her breath. I took a deep breath and reached back, knowing exactly what I'd find.

Perhaps the most extreme example of my malfunctions traumatized an entire Pentecostal Holiness family. My boyfriend wanted to get an iced tea and a sausage biscuit at McDonald's for breakfast. I don't usually eat at McDonald's but he wanted me to go in with him that day.

Before we left I changed out of my pajamas into an ankle length one piece tube top dress, with some giant pink panties down below. I wore a pair of water shoes and threw my hair in a bun. I had old mascara under my eyes but chose not to wash it off. I was a genuine spectacle that morning. I sat down at a table by myself while my boyfriend went off to make his order.

A nice little family of Pentecostals sat directly across the way. They appeared to be a grandma and grandpa, along with their grandson, who looked to be around age thirteen. All three wore the clearly identifiable style of old fashioned Holiness people. I straightened myself up and made sure I didn't do anything to offend them. My boyfriend had his back to me and I started to feel a bit impatient. When I abruptly stood up to go ask him for the keys I stepped on the hem of my dress. There was no hesitation, no time to adjust; my entire dress fell in one motion directly to the floor.

The old man blushed and turned his head to look out the window. The boy stared down at his breakfast with his mouth open. The grandma looked directly at me, pointed and began to laugh. Not just an embarrassed giggle but an outright guffaw. I bent over and pulled the dress back up and tried my best to apologize to the family. Something in that boy's eyes told me he'd never look at an Egg McMuffin in quite the same way, ever again. I'm sorry, boy.

My infamous odd mac muffin was bound to go international at some point. I'm sorry to say Africa was the sad witness to this one. After our long sojourns through the countryside the women of the village and I would gather back at the place of worship, a hut really, with dirt floors and a thatched roof. Sunlight shone through the slats in the walls and rough-hewn benches lined the sparse open space. They had two choirs, one for the men and one for the women. We sang spirituals while we walked for miles across the red dirt land and once we'd reach any village center we'd dance while all the people gathered around. People dropped their chores to see what the fuss was about. I'm no dancer, far from it. But for some reason my dancing became a bit of a sensation across the countryside, perhaps because not many other Americans performed the tribal dances. But man, I got down. I didn't feel awkward or self-aware like I did when I danced in front of my friends in the United States. The beat of the songs and the drums drove me and I just let it all loose. The people were amused and delighted. Some found my dancing hilarious. Screams of delight rose up from the children. I know some of the people were laughing at me because it was just so strange, but I didn't care at all. I felt absolutely free and my body responded in kind.

We headed back into the city and one of the other interpreters told me that word about my walks across the countryside had begun to spread to far away villages. People were telling stories. I felt humbled that I might have connected with people to the extent they wanted to tell their friends. It gave me a measure of confidence that I was indeed following my calling for the right purpose. I asked the interpreter if they were talking about my discussions with them about Jesus. He just smiled and said, "No. The say there is a big white dancer traveling through. They say you dance like you are not even that fat." I took it as a compliment and only winced a teensy bit.

As the days progressed the crowds that came to watch us dance grew bigger and bigger. I made a real spectacle of myself. But I watched the reactions of the women and children who danced with me and I could see they were joyful to include me amongst their ranks. So I just kept dancing.

On our last full day in Malawi all the little village churches gathered in the Holy Dwelling Place, located in Lilongwe. Each village would perform in front of a great crowd of hundreds of people. It was a special treat for our people from the village choir to take a trip on a bus into the big city. Since I'd grown up in the country I knew something about what that felt like. We rode into town packed shoulder to shoulder. I held the littlest girl from the choir on my lap. We sang songs all the way into town and a palpable buzz of energy ran through us as though we were one body.

Several choirs went up before ours. A murmur ran

through the crowd when I got up with my girls and we stomp danced in formation past all the onlookers to a great open area up front. Our Director began a chant and we began to dance and sing, dropping low and thrusting our hips back and forth. I knew the moves to every song and gave every ounce of built up energy I'd shared with the girls on the ride up. As we went through the dance I heard gasps and laughter in the crowd. I glanced at my sisters. They were ecstatic.

Since it was my last day I was down to my very last pair of clean panties for the trip. They were the last pair because they weren't two sizes too big as per my preference. They were two sizes too small and not very cooperative. I noticed out of the corner of my eye that the preacher of Holy Dwelling Place, a sober, serious and wise man was seated behind me and to the left. As we pounded our feet and shook our bodies to the rhythm a terrible realization came over me.

My panties were slowly but predictably falling off. I knew

without a doubt before we made it through our dance,

they'd be rolled up around my ankles. I tried to nonchalantly

hang onto the top of the hem and yank them back up into

place through the fabric of my dress but this kind of dance

requires the use of the entire body. It was no use. I

considered whether I should stop dancing and leave the

performance, but I knew it would be a huge disappointment

to my friends. In the end I decided to just let 'em go.

When we began to dance I noticed the sober Malawi

preacher allowed himself a slight, but detectable smile of

amusement. But as he realized, along with that great cloud of

witnesses that my undergarments were falling off, his

amusement understandably began to wane. When the dance

came to an end the panty descent had reached its inevitable

conclusion. There they were, a sad faded jumble of granny

panty right there on the floor of the church. I glanced back at

the pastor and he had turned away, his gaze upon the wall. I

don't know if he turned away out of respect for me or for his

wife, or if he was just disgusted. I suspect a combination of

the three. To all the people in the world who've involuntarily

been exposed to my odd Mac Muffin, this is where I submit

my sincere apology. You didn't deserve that.

Ride The Bus

The prophetic dreams began in the first

grade. My parents moved us back to Oklahoma from South

Georgia after Dad spent a few years serving in the Army. I

don't remember too much about Georgia, just a few

vignettes here and there, dad catching a little shark in the

ocean, riding my bike around and around our circle drive,

saying Piggly Wiggly all the time and smoking my first

cigarette (I ralphed and cried).

It was 1984 and I was already enchanted with music.

Mom played the radio all the time in the car and our favorite

song was Billy Ocean's Lover Boy. We loved to watch the

music video on MTV with all the space alien creatures

fighting in a bar and then frolicking on a beach. It was like

magic. We still know every single word to that song and

might've coordinated our own dance routine to it a couple of

years ago.

Mom drove us to school every morning because Dad

was in training and we didn't get to see him all that much.

She always decked us out in her jewelry and made sure we

dressed up in pretty clothes every day. My kindergarten

teacher was Mrs. Smiley, and that's a fact. I wanted to be

friends with everyone but spent a lot of time off daydreaming by myself.

When we moved back to our Okie home I'd picked up an extremely heavy southern drawl, which is markedly different from Okie-speak. My parents have a home video from Christmas where I open a present and find a microscope, complete with slides already fixed with insects for viewing. Upon inspection of one particular slide, I read the insect's description, looked directly into the camera and said, "Ahoe, mah luuk, eetsa butterflah frum Saouth Aist Ayshya." Sound it out as it reads and you get the picture.

My accent made me a little different as well as the new kid, so it took a while for all the kids to accept me. But I didn't care, I loved my new school, Westville. I especially loved my teacher, Mrs. Kirk, the same first grade teacher who'd taught my Dad. I tended to annoy most adults because I asked a lot of questions. I mean, I didn't really hold any conversations at all, I just asked question after question. I felt keenly aware there was much to know and I didn't know any of it yet. Mrs. Kirk reassured me it was good to ask questions. She may have come to regret that later, I don't know.

Mrs. Kirk also encouraged my creative bent. She challenged me to fashion a guitar out of a cardboard box and some rubber bands as an evening project on my own. I was to write a song, learn to play the guitar and debut the song in front of the entire class. After school I worked away every night until I was satisfied with my playing and writing skills in anticipation of my stage debut. I went to the front of the class and plucked away at my cardboard box, pluck, pluck, twang, the style was more Saouth Aist Aysia than anything else, to be honest. When I was finished only one person in the entire group applauded. It was old Mrs. Kirk. Nevertheless, I couldn't get enough of school and popped up every morning excited and ready to go. But then came the morning when I woke up from a dream and flat refused to get out of bed.

My parents demanded to know the problem. "I had a dream the school bus crashed and I'm not getting on the bus today. Someone's going to be hurt." I was filled with dread, a feeling to which I was not accustomed.

"Don't be silly, it's just a dream. You can't miss school."

I slunk out from under the covers and pulled on my clothes. Grabbed my backpack and slung it over my shoulder. I didn't argue with my parents so I dragged myself down the gravel driveway and waited at the stop sign with my little sister, Boog. It began to rain. My anxiety grew as the bus wound around its route on snaky Highway 62, taking on more and more kids. The rain came down in sheets. I huddled behind the seat, protecting myself. My eyes just peeped over the top of the green canvas of the next bench, watching the road for what I knew would be coming there. We reached the final curve before we would arrive safe at school and I began to ease up a bit. Perhaps it really had been just a silly dream, I thought, as I looked out the window and saw my friend Beth step out on her porch. She was a little later than usual out to the bus due to her rain gear, I suppose. Out of the corner of my eye I caught movement. Crazy, chaotic, terrifying movement. It was a sedan coming down that steep curve in the rain and the driver had lost control. I watched it careen from one side of the road to the other, the driver frantic and jerking back and forth on the steering wheel in a desperate attempt to stop what he already knew was coming.

The car rammed head on into the school bus traveling around fifty miles per hour. The driver and an infant in the sedan were both badly hurt. Everyone on the bus was ok, save for a few cases of whiplash. Thankfully my friend Beth never made it across the hundred yard walk from her porch to the bus before the crash happened.

The school called our parents to come pick up all the children involved in the accident. Most were emotional and stressed, crying when mom or dad arrived to cart them home. Not me. When my folks arrived I stood with my arms crossed and my head cocked a bit to the side. They wouldn't quite look me in the eye. I thought then it must've been due to their feelings of guilt for failing to listen. The reason may better be attributed to the full realization they were growing one really weird girl.

Remain Silent and Fail Your Friend

After WBF and I graduated law school she went to work as the CFO for her family's manufacturing company. She hired me on a contractual basis to work in-house on employment law and compliance issues. I'd never been in any environment like that before. Sparks flew, grinders screamed, thick smoke hung in the air. It was a difficult adjustment for a softie like me.

One of the first people to make me feel more at ease was a girl who did secretarial work in the front office named

Mandy. She had long thick brown hair that she must have kept in hot rollers because it always held a lovely wave. Her eyes were green and sparked with attitude. She had a strong southern drawl and she used the most colorful expression in her speech. One of her favorites was, "It don't make a shit." She was crass and never tried to put on airs. That made me feel right at home.

Mandy made a habit every morning of bringing her breakfast into my office to sit down and chat. She was a real talker and most of the time she just talked about her large menagerie of animals: a ferret, a rabbit, a snake, several cats and dogs, a caiman. She was passionate for her animals in a way I'd rarely seen in anyone before. She'd survived a rough and unstable childhood but after a couple of failed marriages at a young age she settled down with a new husband. This guy was a former police officer and anytime I was around he never said a word, but I felt he regarded me with some sort of suspicion. He was a quiet man but always sharply observing his surroundings with an eagle's eye constantly on Mandy.

Over time Mandy began to divulge disturbing details about her marriage. She confided that her husband was possessive and jealous of everyone, including her female friends. He began to display abnormal behavior that to me seemed evident of a serious mental disorder. This behavior was clearly in the stalker category. I found it difficult to comprehend. Why would a man stalk his own wife, with whom he worked and went home every night? Mandy said he insisted on constant supervision and knowledge of her whereabouts. She told me he stole and hid her lingerie and that he placed tiny strings on drawers and doors in the house so he would know her movements within the home if he happened to be out. Mandy said they'd had a huge fight because she discovered him locked up in a room hiding one night watching porn.

I'd never heard of anything so crazy. I was unqualified to give relationship advice but on this matter I felt compelled to sound an alarm. I told her to pack up her things, bring her children and leave immediately. I offered her a room at my condo to stay while she filed for divorce until she could save up enough money on her own to find a place. Mandy considered my offer and even drove up to Norman where I lived to see my place. When she came she brought a house-warming gift. A brown pair of woven metal candle holders fashioned in the shape of wine goblets. When lit, the holders threw fantastic shadows on the walls. Shadows! The light spilled out not from the top but from the open spaces between the looping wires around the sides. I knew she didn't have any money to a afford a gift at all, so the light that shone out warmed my heart and reminded me of her generosity every time I saw it.

She left that day and a couple of weeks went by. I didn't push her on the issue of leaving her husband. I knew she had concerns for her kids, for her animals and I knew she loved her husband. I had made the decision to divorce a few years before that and I knew it was a personally devastating experience. I didn't want her to feel any more stress or anxiety than she already felt. Her conversations turned to God. She told me she was an atheist but from her words I gathered that she was angry. Angry for her lost childhood, angry at the abuse, angry about the pain. I was enduring my own spiritual doubts at the time, and though I felt a strong inner compulsion to discuss my faith with her I chose not to. I only listened and did not judge. I knew she could find guidance and strength in a personal relationship with God but I myself was not strong enough in my own faith to help her.

I sat at my condo in Norman on a weeknight when I felt an unsteady feeling. It was a distinct and overwhelming dread. I called all my family members to check on them that night. Everyone was fine. I turned on some music and drank a lot of wine to numb the sick feeling I could not shake. I should have prayed instead.

The next morning I woke up hung-over and I was late getting to the office. Instead of showering to wash off my foggy state I threw on my dress suit and heels, brushed my teeth, pulled my hair back in a greasy ponytail and rushed down I-35, with plans to remain in my office all day and avoid contact with any of my colleagues. I didn't want any of them to witness my disgraceful state. As I exited the interstate and turned onto the state highway the local newsman broke in over the classic rock station I listened to every day.

"A local woman was found strangled Thursday morning. The body of Mandy White was discovered in her home by police. Billy White was arrested in connection with the murder."

I pulled into the plant parking lot and sat like a rock staring out the windshield. I didn't believe it. I wouldn't believe it. It had to be someone else. I gathered up my briefcase and rushed into the front office so I could find Mandy there and know it was all a terrible mistake. I didn't cry. I strode in and addressed our receptionist. She had a pitiful look on her face.

"Is it TRUE?" I pled with my eyes for her to answer

no, but she only nodded her head in sorrow.

I felt like I'd stepped into a different dimension. All of time moved in slow motion. I made my way upstairs and passed the office of our salesman without a word. He must have made a couple of calls when he saw my state because not five minutes passed before the Plant Manager and the Vice President came to my office. I sat there trying to process everything desperate to hold it together but when they walked in I exploded. I wailed and the previously restrained tears poured out in rivers.   I wept without reservation and cried out for mercy. My colleagues were at a loss themselves but both came over and put their arms around me. I pushed them both away and yelled out, "SHE NEVER EVEN HAD A CHANCE!" I think I was waiting for some kind of explanation in response, but there was nothing to offer. In hindsight I think I was making a declarative statement and my friends understood that I needed to say it. It was just the truth and remains so, then and now.

I've spent hours untold thinking about what I might've done differently during that time. I allowed myself to become bitter and angry. I turned my back on the truth with intent, not willing to look in the mirror and accept responsibility. I was in a dark period and allowed my spiritual self to wither away to almost nothing. My choices and weaknesses were human but I also knew the way out, I just chose not to seek it. I could have given Mandy an answer. I could have led her to a gift. But instead I failed my friend. I pray that she forgives me and that her Father will, too. I let both of them down with the sin of silence.

I've moved so many times since we lost our friend and every time I do, I leave behind most of my earthly possessions. It feels good to just give them away. Starting

over and getting born again is one thing I've become adept at

over time. But no matter where I run I keep those wire

candleholders close by. I like to burn candles in them and

watch the light and shadow fight with each other up there on

the wall. The light serves as a constant reminder I can always

do better.

Scribble Some Notes

An Interlude

She slept a languorous sleep interwoven with vanishing dreams, abandoned to fate and indifferent to consequences.

It's A Dream: We were in some tourist town. You walked in and we sat side stage while a band played. They were all dressed up in sparkly suits. One of them started playing a Leon Russell song. You walked onstage, stopped the music to show them how to play it correctly. Then you just came right back over and sat down again.

It's A Dream: I still have dreams about him and that infuriates me. I can't see him but I know he's there. After a month or so another man began to appear in the dreams. I don't know him yet but he is kind and good. I always end up leaving with him. Always.

It's A Dream: Our first date was Friday the 13th. That night I dreamt a vision of us standing together. All the seasons passed by in just a few moments. Winter to spring, a hot summer and finally the leaves began to fall, red and gold all around. I took that to mean we would last through it all; never fall apart. Now I understand what it meant. We would end when next the leaves were burned with frost.

It's Murphy's Law:

Anything that can go wrong does go wrong.
Malignity of Matter

Total depravity of inanimate things

"Whatever can happen will happen if we make trials enough." ~Augustus de Magan

It's Loretta Lynn:

"If you write it down, it don't hurt so bad." ~Loretta Lynn

It's Steve Ripley

"Dreamed a corset and a buffalo

And a midget boxing kangaroo from Hong Kong

You were there standing on a hilltop smiling

Closer to right than wrong

Yellow was a crime against the state

But the Ladies Auxiliary got the law repealed

Magic is jive just like jive is magic

The Wizard of Oz is finally revealed

Traded away my special orange sauce

For a brief glimpse of Richard Burton

You said it was all dash and folly

Pay no attention to that man behind the curtain"

~Original lyrics composed by Steve Ripley, ©2013

It's A Prayer: The water at my feet. Did it travel so far only to arrive in this place, kiss the sand and turn back? Now is the time when the difference between the ocean and the sky cannot be perceived. A time when the blackest of nights commission the brightest of stars. Just discern the whitecaps as they break and advance on the shoreline. The sight seizes my body with an unforeseen fear. I pray for those hearts so far across the water and implore them to pray in return; that I may never forget the things I have seen; that I might never go numb, but forever feel the heat of a fervent passion and never fear the pain it must bring; that this life is lived with the heart of a servant; that I will never be the same. And these waves, they just keep coming

Repel An Asian Woman

WBF took me on the most opulent vacation of my life. We toured San Francisco and Napa Valley then flew to Hawaii where we would cruise around to spend a day on every island. Now, I was raised a Baptist girl, which means I'm a real prude at heart. I also have some kind of mental disorder, if you will, in which I highly dislike intimate physical contact, not just from strangers but from anyone. My own family has a ball sitting too close or forcing me to hug. The pat's better. A hug is just so, ugh it's just so very CLOSE. I always feel weird and awkward. I love people, honest I do, it's just…no touchie, please. This condition rules with such force that I loathe manicures, pedicures and massages. A total stranger rubbing oil all over with naught but a thin sheet of cloth covering my lady bits? No thanks.

But WBF insisted on booking a massage for me as a special treat. I looked in the spa menu and noted that it was rather pricey at well over $200. That amount of money equaled almost half my rent on which I happened to be late at that moment. So, I steeled myself with two glasses of champagne and walked up to the spa level.

They sent me back to a darkened room that smelled of spice and eucalyptus. I heard the sounds of running water and mandolins over the speakers. Everything was immediately weird and off-putting. A tiny bird-like lady walked in. She couldn't have weighed ninety pounds. As first I thought maybe they'd sent a third grade girl in to do the work.

"Good afternoon," she crooned in a sweet, high-pitched voice.

"Hi, how are ya," I croaked back, feeling very much trapped and cornered by this little lady.

She held out a robe and the tiniest pair of paper-string panties I'd ever seen in my life. I clutched them to my chest.

"The massage you've selected today is called the Citrus Scrub. It's a de-toxifying concoction. I'll be applying the scrub to your entire body. So before we start, I'll ask you to get in the shower and clean yourself. Afterwards, please towel off and lie face up on the table."

My eyes bugged out of my head.

"What about the sheet?" I implored. My mouth hung open in disbelief.

"This is a detox scrub for the entire body. It's important to apply it on the midsection. So please no sheet."

In shock I made my way to the shower and contemplated my options. Could I run? And if so, where to? I was stranded on a floating boat in the middle of the Pacific Ocean. They would track me down. I knew I could physically overpower this woman but then how would that look during my arraignment for assault and battery? "DRUNKEN ZAFTIG AMAZON ATTACKS TINY SPA EMPLOYEE JUST TRYING TO DO HER JOB". I was frantic. So I decided to do what I always do when faced with a situation in which I should absolutely stand up for myself and my own personal convictions: I pretended like it wasn't happening and went to my imaginary happy place. I stepped out of the shower and like a robot, toweled off, walked over and ratcheted my big naked ass up on that table. I laid back and closed my eyes, for I did not want to see.

Shortly I felt tiny little hands fluttering over my exposed skin, rubbing a citrus-salt concoction into my pores. I thought to myself, "God, please don't let her say anything, oh please, I'm begging, please don't let this lady say anything to me."

Several minutes went by in silence, save for the plucking mandolin. She reached my mid-section and poked around at my fleshy middle.

"Oh, you have alcohol in your system," she said in her delightful little lilt. "Oo, you SO FAT! Why you kill you self?"

When it was all over I jumped into my clothes, thanked her for the worst experience of my life and ran straight out of that den of torture. As I emerged I saw WBF there, fresh out of her own naked massage, with a beaming smile that lit up her face in an expression of what can only be described as exalted joy.

Replace Mick Jagger

A note I shared with my friends just before I left for Africa:

I was thinking my tomatoes wouldn't be ready before I left but my sister gave me a little red one that had ripened early when I stopped in to tell my family goodbye. It tasted salty - like home. Walked in and Dad was listening to Not Dark Yet. Criminy, emotions are intense today. Ndiri Bwino (I am fine) but maybe in my heart ndanyamuka (I have already departed). It all begins tomorrow. Prepared. Send your love and I promise to carry it with me over the ocean and pour it out upon some red dirt not so different from Oklahoma.

My life began to change the moment I deplaned in Africa. I hadn't yet made it to my final destination, for we had to refuel in the Ethiopian capital, Addis Ababa. I'd worked for some time in a manufacturing plant where welders built equipment for oil fields. The first time I walked in the plant, with sparks flying, buzzsaws whirring, hoists lifting tons of steel in the air and welders soldering, every nerve in my body instantly lit up on alert. I became hyper-aware of my surroundings to the smallest detail. I think that must be some kind of evolutionary survival mechanism. When a human finds herself in unidentifiable environs she probably ought to pay attention to detail. I felt that again in Addis.

Everything I saw, smelled, heard and felt was completely distinct from any previous life experience. I had zero stored references to serve as a guide. My body went tingly all over and my skin rose up with goose bumps. The smell in the Addis airport was earthy, strong and human. I told myself to be cool but it was impossible. I found myself staring at everything all at once, trying to drink it all in. No one appeared to notice my presence. Travelers rushed past on a mission to get home, or to get away, everyone trying to get somewhere. All except for one boy riding on his mother's back in a sling. His mother stood tall and strong; a beautiful woman wearing a head wrap. Her cheekbones were delicate and high and her eyes were almond shaped. I gazed at her beauty and she never noticed, but her son did. He made direct eye contact. It's difficult to explain what I saw in that baby's eyes. I knew immediately he understood something I did not. He'd seen some things I'd never get to see. His eyes appeared old and wise. He held my gaze until his mother walked off into the massive throng of travelers. After he disappeared I accepted that the coming experience would be one to change my entire life and my whole world perception.

We boarded the plane and made our last leg of the trip for Malawi. A short flight of only four hours, compared to the exhausting trans-Atlantic flight I'd just endured. We landed and took a bus to our living quarters for the next two weeks, a place called Nellie's Guest House, which I counted as a good luck sign since my nickname is Nellie. The next morning I met my interpreter and we drove out for a couple of hours into the country to meet the village where I'd be based. The people were waiting when I arrived, who knows for how long. The ground was unsettled by all their feet and a great cloud of red dirt surrounded them. They immediately brought me inside their rugged hut of a worship place. Someone guided me to a place right up front and the huge crowd filed in to sit on the little planks of wood that served as pews. I sat very still but my eyes roamed over the crowd, taking in every face and every emotion. The church leader walked up and handed me an orange Fanta. My friend and the leader of the American group, Brother Johnny, leaned over and explained that a Fanta was the equivalent of a day's working wages for the villagers. I didn't want to drink it. I looked out at all those faces, many desperately thin and malnourished, and I wanted to give it back. I wanted to beg them to each take a sip until it was gone. I knew if I refused it would insult everyone who'd sacrificed to give a gift to their guests. So I sat there, a spoiled, fat, ungrateful American, and I drank that orange Fanta while dozens of hungry eyes watched every sip. I thought of one of my favorite novels, Heart of Darkness by Joseph Conrad. I feared the message I might send to their culture as well as the wake I might leave when I departed.

One of my assignments in Malawi was to work with the children. When I learned of this I felt offended. First of all, I don't consider myself much of a 'kid' person. My own child is a delight but he spoke like an adult from an early age and conducted himself in much the same way. I considered the implications of why I'd been relegated to the kids' class.

Was it because I'm a woman? Perhaps because I was new to the church and considered a rookie? Self-doubt plagued my preparation for the trip. I began to worry about our influence on the Malawian culture. Would we ultimately serve as colonialists, Americanizing a vibrant native culture? The horror of that possibility was potent because of the trials of my own Cherokee ancestors. I questioned my motivations and the motivations of the group. I forgot about that little 'push' I'd felt that day in church when the preacher asked the congregation to examine their hearts for a call.

One of the first people I encountered once I reached the village was a boy named Chisomo. He was beautiful and shy, around twelve years old, and seemed to be the leader of all the other children. He was assigned to accompany me while we walked from village to village. Chisomo immediately took the bag I'd carried out to the bush. It must have weighed twenty pounds, stuffed with treats for the kids I'd meet later, my Bible, plenty of bottled water and a giant bag of pistachios. I was horrified. It felt like a confirmation of my previous doubts. Here was this little boy whose clothes hung in tatters, no shoes on his feet, carting around my fat American bag. I tried to plead with him through the interpreter, explaining that I could carry my own bag.

"Please Son, walk with me. But let me carry my own bag. I am strong enough."

Despite his shyness, Chisomo would not relent on this issue. He remained at my side walking for miles and miles carrying that bag without a single complaint.

I thought about what I might tell the Malawian children. What stories could I share with them given the vast differences in our cultures? How could they relate to someone like me considering the burgeoning excess at home

and the stark absence of material comfort in their own

villages? I imagined they would only perceive me to be some

overstuffed great white weirdo.

But I was so wrong. Only one small toddler saw me

and cried, but I understood completely. It must have been

disturbing to see something so different. A thing that doesn't

look like it belongs anywhere in the world as you've known it

to this point. Akin to the first time you take your child to the

mall to see an adult dressed up like a giant Easter Bunny.

(Stop doing that, you guys, it's a pretty twisted tradition.) The

rest of the children were enthralled. They flocked around in

giant crowds jostling each other about to hold my hand. The

girls wanted to braid my hair. I felt a bit like the pied piper as

I walked across the countryside in the midst of that great

throng of smiling, singing little faces.

Chisomo remained ever at my side. He watched out for me in his shy way, this young man who insisted on carrying my bag. When the crowds of children became too boisterous and shoving broke out Chisomo gently intervened until calm was restored. He was a natural leader of the children. We forged a strong bond together as a team. I asked him, "Chisomo, if you could go anywhere in the whole world and be anything you wanted, what would be your choice?"

"A bus driver," came the quiet reply.

I stewed and prayed over the correct story to tell them and at last I came to an answer. I'd tell them a story about my farm. I'd just moved back to Adair County to finish writing my first novel. I moved in with my baby sister and her husband, who'd just bought a little hobby farmhouse. The first thing we did was hit up the local co-op to pick out a dozen or so baby chicks. Even though we were country folk we'd never raised birds before and had no idea how to tell the baby hens from baby roosters. So, we ended up with about a fifty-fifty percentage. Not a great idea for a farmyard.

We named our birds after rock stars*. Goose Springsteen, Freddie Mercury, Simon and Garduckel, etc. One of the roosters was particularly aggressive. I named him Mick Jagger. He was obviously proud of his appearance and cornered the market on the lady birds. Since everyone else worked a 9-5 job, my responsibility was caring for the animals. I went out and gave them water and food every morning before I started writing. Mick Jagger and I struck up quite a repertoire. Eventually, no one else could go out to feed the animals without Mick flogging them. He developed quite an impressive cock-a-doodle-doo and he let that sucker

loose all day long. Mick Jagger was The Man.

Shortly before I was to leave for Africa I went out in

the barnyard at dusk to check the birds. All the rock stars had

made it into their coop except for Mick. Very unusual since

he never left the girls to themselves before. He still sat

perched on his favorite spot – the top of the dog house. I was

worried he'd be eaten in the night so I tried to catch him.

This frightened Mick, as I'd never violated his space before.

He squawked off running and flapping out into the field as

fast as he could. I forgot all about the other chickens and

took out after him through the darkening hayfield but I

couldn't catch him. So I went back and got a flashlight. I hiked

out in the middle of the field to a small pond, but spotted

nary a feather. I feared the worst. Finally I walked back into

the forest located several hundred yards behind the house. I knew if I found him out there he would be dead. At last I spotted something white up in a tree. It was Mick. When we spotted each other he cocked his head and eyed me a little as if to be sure the coast was clear. Then he fluttered down off his branch and walked back home with me. Maybe it's better to say I walked and he strutted.

When I told the village children my farm story I let each of them know they were just like Mick Jagger in the heart of the Creator. "Listen, you are each special with your very own unique gifts. You're considered precious. You're loved deeply. You're loved so much that your Father sent me across the ocean to make sure you knew."

I had no idea how that story would translate but as my interpreter explained that they were each special and loved, I saw shining beams break out in the crowd. Lots of giggles and smiles. The only exception was Chisomo. He had a strange look of distress and concern on his face. I felt like his mysterious, loyal heart was empathizing with me on some level.

Sometimes I get to speak to kids about writing here in the United States and when I tell them they're unique, special and loved they react in the same manner. On this matter I found that nothing is lost in translation. Every child should hear it out loud: "Look kid, you need to know you're just like Mick Jagger."

On my last day in the village following the emotional last sermon, I hugged my friends and tried to get to each of them one last time. I felt like I needed to touch them and store up their tremendous, powerful love until I could return. We'd forged a real kinship. I felt the same grief leaving them as when I'd left my family in the United States. I knew they had to get back to everyday life as I also had to return to mine. I'd interrupted their lives enough. But I was in pain.

We slowly moved through the crowd toward the white mini-bus that would return us to Lilongwe and ultimately, the airport. I searched through the crowd for Chisomo but for the first time since my arrival he was nowhere to be seen. I couldn't imagine leaving without embracing my loyal son one last time. But we were short on time, already late, and Brother John expressed urgency that we get on the road to make one last ceremony at the Holy Dwelling Place. When I reached the bus I turned around to make one last wave. When I did so, I noticed the crowd had begun to part and in the midst of all those faces I spotted Chisomo. He held something close to his chest and walked toward me with a determined look in his eye. When he came close I saw that he held a rooster snuggled in his arms. It was by far the finest rooster I'd ever seen in my entire life. Of all the scraggly, chewed-up, desperate-looking chickens I'd seen running for their lives in all the villages, this one was clearly a prized possession. His sleek black feathers gleamed iridescent green and purple when hit by the sunlight. Chisomo spoke to the interpreter as he gently passed the rooster into my arms. He said, "Because you have lost your rooster we want you to take ours."

I took the rooster and held it close so it would remain calm. Then I stood there stunned and overwhelmed. I would never go hungry in my life. None of my family members would either. We are poor by American standards but by the world's standard we live in gross overabundance. The parents in this village couldn't have guaranteed their children would have a source of protein that night. But they allowed their children to bring me the finest rooster in the land. In their constant struggle to survive they found generosity and empathy to replace something I'd lost. It amounted to the most monumental, selfless and valuable gift I've received in forty years on earth. Brother John said in all his time of service in Malawi he'd never witnessed such a thing. That rooster changed my life forever.

Exhibit C

Make A Fowl Inventory

1. Goose Springsteen – African Goose
2. Fleetwood Quack – African Goose
3. Paul Simon – White Crested Duck
4. Art Garduckel – Black Crested Duck
5. Ziggy Stardust – Red Rooster Nekkid Neck
6. Spyder From Mars (Spydie) – Red Nekkid Neck

7. Ike Turner – Black Astrolorp
8. Tina Turner – Black Astrolorp
9. Sammy Davis, Jr – Black Polish
10. Dean Martin – White Polish
11. Red Molly – Production Red
12. Mick Jagger – White Austrolorp
13. Lady Blue – Americauna
14. The Hoff – German Silver
15. Bob Dylan – German Silver
16. Neil Young – German Silver
17. Tom Jones – Red Bourbon Turkey (sex unsettled)
18. Frank Beard – Red Banty
19. Dusty Bill – Black Feathered Foot
20. Billy Chickens – White Feathered Foot

Crush On Louis CK

After I published my first novel I decided to go on a

little self-promotional book tour. WBF decided we should

take a swipe at the east coast. We decided on Philadelphia,

Atlantic City and New York City. I'd never been to any place

out east except for Washington, D.C. After I wrapped up a

few local book signing events in Oklahoma we took out on

another grand adventure. WBF left me in charge of planning

our itinerary. We sailed the Delaware in Philadelphia on a

boat with an on-board wine and cheese tasting. I'd carefully

wrapped and packed a bottle of Rubicon all the way from

Oklahoma for the occasion. Then we went to a museum of

medical oddities where I spent hours ogling weird things in

jars. By the way, did you know that a hairball the size of a

watermelon was once removed from a human stomach?

Fascinating.

Our next stop was Atlantic City. We checked into our

hotel and found ourselves in a teeming crowd of green.

Heineken was holding their corporate convention in our

hotel. Everywhere I went I encountered some drunken,

leering executive harping about marketing this, promotional that. WBF and I went to sit at the bar while we waited on our table at the in-house restaurant.

The bartender caught my eye right off the bat. He was a ginger, not that I prefer red-heads necessarily, but it just so happens that I have a ridiculous crush on the comedian Louis C.K. I have it bad for David Letterman too, especially the newly-retired, bald and bearded Letterman in jogging shorts. But I consider C.K. brilliant. An observational genius. Brutally truthful and a real jerk. It's a lethal combination in my wheelhouse. I never dated a bald or balding guy until I discovered Louis but after that it sort of opened up the bald guy floodgates in my life. They just kept rolling in somehow. I like to close my eyes, rub that waxy hairless acreage and pretend it's ole Louis there.

I told the ginger bartender I thought he looked like Louis C.K. He'd never heard of Louis C.K., to my great surprise. Nevertheless he took that as a sign of interest and started to get pretty chummy with me. Before too awful long the ginger asked for my cell number. I was flattered and WBF was annoyed. When the time arrived for our table reservation we asked for the tab but he comped us and said, "a couple of girls like you should never have to pay for a tab." I giggled something stupid and floated on imaginary daisies all the way to dinner.

After dinner I went up to my room, a little bored. WBF always insists on separate hotel rooms because she's a freakin' princess and the pea and I snore like a wasted cow swallowed an accordion. I decided I'd harass my little sister, like De Niro says, 'a lil bit'. She was keenly aware of my avid affection for Louis CK. So I sent her a text that read, "you won't believe who just bought me a drink in Atlantic City."

Her reply was instantaneous. "WHO?" I sent back, "Louis

C.K." The phone rang within an instant after I hit the send

button.

"You did NOT," she spat, breathless. She demanded

to know every last detail. I snickered to myself and improved

on the spot an audacious, impossible yarn about how Louis

CK had fallen for my charms and asked for a copy of my book.

I hung up the phone and shook my head at her naiveté, then

decided I'd let her stew on it for the night. When we woke up

the next day we took off for New York City and I forgot all

about my fabricated encounter until I made it back home a

week later. Upon arrival I noticed everyone was watching me

with a strange, excited look on their face. My mom couldn't

hold it in any longer and she spouted out, "Did you REALLY

hook up with Louis CK?" My sister had taken a few liberties

of her own with the story and then told the entire family (except maybe not grandma) that Louis CK and I had met. She'd embellished even further and now the entire family became convinced that he and I were an item.

Now listen, I hate lies, really I do, and it's a personal goal of mine to never, ever lie to anyone about anything. But for whatever reason that day, facing their sad excitement that maybe they'd finally marry me off to a real winner, I just couldn't tell them the truth. I let that hideous lie grow and become family legend. Dad was not familiar with Louis CK at that time, but he began regularly watching the FX show Louie. He became convinced that Louis is a genius. Dad developed a bro-crush on Louis CK. He was totally enamored. I'd go over for a visit and he'd have an episode queued up on the DVR – an episode he'd already watched three times.

"Has he emailed you yet?" Dad would ask, eyebrows raised with anticipation.

"No, Dad, haven't heard anything."

"He probably just hasn't had time to finish your book yet. Busy man, that Louis."

"Yeah Dad, he's real busy."

I'd feel guilty and sit down with Dad to watch our ginger-haired amour. Sadly, as of this writing I've still not had the guts to tell my family I never met Louis CK but rather some flame-topped bartender whose name I can't recall in a bankrupt hotel on the Jersey shore. Somewhere out in the Ozark foothills of eastern Oklahoma my dad still waits with his Louie collection. For he believes the day is coming soon when he will call his beloved first-born Faithy CK.

Leave a Chicken Man and

Become the Cherokee Drifter of Your Dreams

After I learned the Chicken Man lied to me I never

felt entirely comfortable with him again. He swore he'd never

lie or hurt me again and began attending therapy sessions.

He finalized his divorce. He pledged his undying love. But

deep down I felt a real conviction that something awful

waited for both of us down the road.

The thing that was different with the Chicken Man

was his uncommon acts of service. He worked hard all the

time. For the first time in my life I found a break in the

constant struggle to make it on my own. I'd spent my adult

years making myself into a capable, independent woman but

for once, it seemed, someone reliable was there to fix my

vehicle when it broke down. I had a partner who happily took care of the lawn work. This was a man who found pleasure in cooking lovely meals for me every night, after I'd become accustomed to beef jerky and canned tuna fish for dinner. When I left out on a vacation with WBF he drove out to my house every day, a two hour round trip, to feed and look after my scraggly dump dogs. He asked to go to all my son's sports events. No suitor had ever gone to such lengths for me, ever. As a feminist I am loathe to say it out loud, but for once I felt a sense of relief that I didn't have to do everything myself. It felt good to be with someone who wanted to take care of me.

I told him I wasn't the kind of person who needed to be together every single day. In fact, I needed to be alone on a regular basis in order to write. I'd been working on my second fiction novel for some time and people were asking about it. During the whirl of our courtship I'd left my one true love, writing, on the backburner. But he wasn't satisfied with seeing me a couple days a week. He wanted us to be together every day.

He began to take vacation days from work to accompany me to my book signings. Book sales were my only source of income. I received a royalty check from Amazon here and there but I paid my rent by appearing at public book signings. After the third book event he attended we drove back to my house and the Chicken Man began to discuss how the book signings weren't financially viable for us as a couple and that we'd be better off if I stayed home and focused on finishing the follow-up fiction novel. He was helping me with rent and adept at financial management, where I had neither skills nor motivation in that area. It didn't take much persuasion before I willingly gave up my only means to support myself financially. I became completely dependent on a person to whom I should never have handed over that power.

After the Chicken Man's divorce became final he took physical possession of his place, which he called "The Ranch". He took me there and showed me where he planned to make a giant vineyard. My Dad had given him many lessons on the art of winemaking and the Chicken Man decided he wanted to build an Oklahoma winery based on what he'd learned. He wanted to invest in and make a wine business. He said it was his dream for himself and the family, and that eventually he would use that as a springboard to leave his full time job. I took that to mean that he genuinely intended on a long term relationship.

He'd already proposed to me once in July, but given

my hesitations, I couldn't agree. Then in October he asked

again but a little voice deep down kept saying, "don't do it,

don't do it, don't do it." Truth is I've been engaged over half

a dozen times and it never stuck anyway, so an engagement

never held much water with me. Finally in December he took

me to the ocean. He wanted to walk out on the pier. I'd been

a difficult customer to get along with that day. It was really

cold and windy out and when we came to the pier I saw that

they charged a fee to walk out on it.

"A *fee* to walk out on a stack of wood piled up in the

ocean?" I railed, even though I knew I wouldn't be the one

footing the bill. "Forget this. I prefer to walk the beach."

But Chicken Man persisted, as was his way, and I

honestly didn't care one way or the other, I just relish an

opportunity to be unreasonable. What did I care if he wanted to waste eight bucks to take a walk on the pier? So we took out on a stroll all the way to the end of the pier where the local fisherman gathered with their ice chests and beer. I got the impression they were serious about the task at hand and didn't appreciate lookie-loos popping up over their shoulder asking, "Any luck?!"

Chicken Man and I put our arms around each other. We leaned over the rail looking out into the vast open ocean. I spotted a tiny bird riding the waves. She disappeared, diving deep into the water. I scanned the surface waiting for her to pop back up. A couple of minutes passed and I felt sure some fanged dweller of the deep had eaten the little thing. But no, she popped back up like a little feathered bobber and continued on diving and surfacing. I stared at the little bird for a very long time, marveling at her bravery, to be such a sweet tiny thing drifting alone out on that vast sea, with all the sharks circling hungry just below.

The Chicken Man said he was ready to start back so we walked the way we'd come, hand in hand. We came to a bench and he asked if I would sit down with him for a bit. We sat side by side and he started talking. I wasn't really paying close attention when he grabbed my left hand and slid a plain black band on my ring finger. I immediately felt bad for complaining about the pier and being a difficult bird, in general. He might've proposed we were about to board a jet-fueled hot dog that would fly us to the planet Uranus and I would've agreed. But instead he asked me to marry him. I said yes, for a lot of reasons that make no sense, but also because I loved him.

After we returned from the engagement journey he started talking about launching the winery, and how we couldn't maintain both of our homes at the same time. I'd

need to move in at the ranch. I resisted that idea but I also

knew it was a financial strain on him, plus he faced pressure

from family members when he came out to my house. They

wanted him nearby.

The owners of my own house contacted me to say

they had potential buyers coming to see my house. I'd

discussed working out a deal to purchase the house with

them previously, but the complications with the relationship

put all that on indefinite hold. The owners, in the wake of my

procrastination, understandably moved on. When I heard

people were coming in to view the home I took it as a sign

that it was time to really commit to the Chicken Man and the

winery dream he had for us. I gave the owners notice that I

would move out in three months but they wrote back that a

deal would close in twenty days. I felt shocked and scared

but began packing my things. My heart was heavy.

I told the Chicken Man I needed time to myself to say goodbye to my place. My identity as a struggling writer was entangled with the lovely, lonely, isolated place out in the woods. It seemed I was leaving a dear old friend for good. The Chicken Man said he understood. I set about getting my books packed into boxes. That's always the most important thing every time I have to move. My books. Everything else I can live without. The books must always go with me.

That night I didn't want to go to bed. I sat in the music room listening to Joe Baxter and The Lost Cause on the record player, spinning my world globe that sat in the middle of the table. I fell asleep on my back just before 2 a.m. on my little loveseat with my long legs hanging off the end.

In the dream I had that night the Chicken Man came

to me in an attempt to reconcile because we were no longer together, for what reason I didn't know. We stood in my open den in front of the stone fireplace and talked. I looked outside the large floor to ceiling windows and saw a giant wine distribution truck pull up in my driveway. It backed in, then took off in the opposite direction. Suddenly I heard a pounding on the window. Outside there stood a Cherokee drifter. He looked to be in bad shape.

"Water," he cried, "please give us water."

The Chicken Man looked at me and said, "Don't do it, Faith. Don't open that door."

But I was already on my way to the kitchen to get a pitcher of water. I turned on the faucet. But when I turned around with the pitcher the Chicken Man staggered in, with a look of wide-eyed shock. His right arm was crossed against his chest.

"What?" I asked, impatient. "What's wrong with you?" I felt annoyed in the dream because the Chicken Man was acting so dramatic.

But he let his arm fall to his side and that's when I saw a massive, jagged piece of glass jutting out from his heart and another from the crook of his arm, stuck right in the vein. He was dying. The Cherokee drifter had stabbed him. I went to him and desperately tried to save his life but to no avail. When I awakened my mouth was so dry it felt glued together. I staggered into the kitchen and poured myself a glass of water. I felt overwhelmed by an impending gloom and pulled on my boots to go walk around outside in the dark. I needed to prove to myself there weren't any drifters out there. Excepting there was. I just didn't know it yet.

I couldn't shake the awful cloud of despair surrounding me, and all just from a dream. I knew it held great significance but all I could do was keep packing and wait to see what was coming. For several years I'd been friends with a man named Bruce on Facebook. We were introduced based on our mutual passion for Neil Young. He often sent articles about meteor showers and ancient Native artifacts. We never met in person but the friendship was real in my view. We spent many hours discussing song lyrics and constellations. He'd always end his messages to me with this line: "Always keep looking up. You never know what's coming down." Bruce passed away several months before and I'd been saddened by the loss.

It was my last night of packing before I was due to start moving my things out to the Chicken Man's ranch. I received a strange notification on my phone from Bruce's

Facebook account. I'd never seen a notification like it before. It led me to an electronic folder full of something called 'filtered messages'. I scrolled through them and found hundreds of messages I'd never seen before. I spotted a message from a woman I didn't know. When I opened the message it read, "Thanks for your post last night. You should know that I've also been dating the Chicken Man since July." She included screenshots of their text message conversations that left no doubt they'd been very intimate for a lengthy period of time. She was begging him to come see her and he was making excuses for why he couldn't. He had confided painfully personal details with her about me and my family.

Shaking, I sent her a reply. "I'm sorry, I've just seen your message. Thank you." Then I sent a message to the Chicken Man to tell him we were over for good. With that incredibly strange twist of fate, I lost my home and became the Cherokee drifter of my dreams.

Pen A Delayed Response

That emotional ambush you left did its damage.

Hadn't you already slashed and burned enough to satisfy the

mocker in your heart? I hope it made you feel better; I hope

some good came from it.

A hastily scribbled note left on the table. Those black

metal engagement rings. Springsteen's Atlantic City playing

on repeat. That was the meanest act of them all, to set it up

so I would walk in my house to find those things. You thought

enough to leave instructions for me along with a

poorly-worded, pithy statement, "I'm sorry I'm a bad man.

You were good to me." Then, "throw our rings in the

reservoir" and "drink the wine for us".

You might've already guessed, but let me confirm here that I failed to follow instruction. The wine you left behind – that bottle of what used to be my favorite Pinot Noir – I never tasted it. I gave it to a couple in love. I promise they didn't waste it on anything so empty and desperate as sentimentality. They told me it did not taste bitter at all.

I gave the black rings to an artist. She melted them down and created something new.

When you wrote to my sisters, "I have tamed The Wild One", you never heard them laugh. They only had to sit back and wait because they know me better than anyone else ever will.

You insisted on making our relationship a spectacle when you knew that made me feel terribly uncomfortable.

You said when people mentioned my name about my books and my dreams they should also say yours. So here, now you get what you want.

You thought to subvert my spirit with words, music and wine? Those things belong to ME. I OWN THEM. So now you see, I've found a few words of my own. I pray you take your Uncle Kracker station, your secret phone lines and your damaged heart and go find fulfillment. But you won't find it without the light. Not the false light, but the light. I wish that for you too, and I forgive you.

See Whatever You Saw

A long procession followed us down to the water.

The closest body of water to the village where I worked is best described as a bog down in a hollow. My interpreter and friend, Shaista, came from a family of successful businesspeople in Lilongwe. Compared to the villagers they were quite comfortable financially. She's a beautiful and charming young woman, quiet, reserved and incredibly poised for her young age. Shaista explained to me that the people in Malawi hold a superstition about the water. Some believe that evil spirits dwell in the depths. When we topped the hill and began our descent toward the bog I understood why.

The reeds and marsh grasses grew waist high in most places. It was a steep drop down to the water and if you weren't careful of your steps descending the slope, it would be easy to find yourself tumbling headfirst into the dark water. Oh, and that's the other thing. Although I'd crossed one or two free-flowing streams in my walks, this water wasn't moving much if at all. The bottom wasn't visible through the murky water, and it only got worse after a few feet got in and started roiling up the sediment. Which brings us to the most pressing concern – alligators. I never saw an alligator in Malawi, but one of the other Americans claimed to have seen one, and the locals told me of a nearby ferryman who'd lost an arm to one.

I'd spent a few years in Georgia when I was young and my parents took us to swim in the lake, a pastime we missed since leaving Oklahoma. Boog and I waded about twenty yards out from the bank. We were splashing around out there, just as we had done in our own creeks and lakes back home, when mom spotted an alligator several hundred yards out, just sitting there, well, floating I suppose, watching us. She told us to get out of the water and we hustled out but when we looked back, the alligator had disappeared. We sat on the bank with our picnic for a bit, keeping an eye on the water, and before long that alligator popped right up in the very spot where we'd played. That stuck with me for a long time. While I can't say I have a real fear of gators, I certainly respect the fact that when you're in their territory, you're fair game and a very real (lesser) member of the food chain.

That experience helped me understand why the villagers held superstitions about the dark water. I theorized that it was based on a survival mechanism stemming from some very real horror that had taken place on those banks generations ago. I was amazed to see the great number of people who walked to the water from miles and miles around to be baptized. It demonstrated a real act of courageous faith.

The scene very much reminded me of my rural Oklahoma family. When my mom decided to be baptized it was a symbolic, serious event with the family and a few members of the little country church in attendance. We gathered on the banks of the creek that ran through our little community. Mom got into Dad's flat-bottom boat, that he'd used hundreds of time before to pull in flat-head catfish off of trotlines, and he paddled to the opposite side, where the preacher-man stood waiting in the sunlight to submerge her in the same place where she'd laughed and swum and caught crawdads as a little girl. It was quite a contrast to the baptism/bouncy house mega-church events in the cities. Not that there's anything wrong with that. The rural experiences suit my spiritual needs best, that's all.

The Malawi baptisms were just like that. A sense of great peace and tight community reigned, a real spirit of brotherhood and sisterhood ran through the crowd. I stood

on the far bank from the place where the people entered the

water. After each person was baptized I would greet and

embrace them and help them up the steep bank. I don't

know how many people came up out of the water that day,

but they just seemed to keep coming for hours. Each person

emerged with a broad smile and a shiver, holding on tight as

we held each other and walked up the bank.

My attention was called to a particular woman as she

approached the water. Her body language was different and I

noticed she looked stiff, distinctly at odds from the others.

She began to shake and as the preacher prayed her body

went into convulsions. It appeared to be a real medical

emergency. Several men carried her out of the water while

her body writhed and jerked in extreme duress. They carried

the woman up and laid her beneath a Mulanje cypress tree. I

abandoned my position and ran up the hill to kneel at her side in the dirt. I was taken aback by what I saw. Her eyes lolled back in their sockets so that only the whites were visible. Her muscles were locked in spasms that caused her arms, wrists, and fingers to draw up in a clawed position. Frothy white spittle foamed out of her mouth. My immediate instinct was to tilt her head back and attempt to clear the airway, but beyond that I had no emergency response training. I am the only attorney in a family of medical professionals for a reason. I don't respond well to emergencies or unexpected body fluid.

After I saw that her airway was cleared I rocked backward on my haunches and looked around for help, unsure what to do. I was in a state of shock. Women from the villages had gathered around, and they seemed to be looking to me for an answer. Shaista waited by my side and I looked at her, a girl half my age, for an answer. Shaista did not appear alarmed at all and in her quiet, assured manner, she said, "I think it is time for you to pray." Of course, of course, I had come there to pray, after all. So while the convulsions continued I placed my hand on her shoulder and began to pray out loud while Shaista translated for the women who stood around us. I still can't remember the words that came out of my mouth. I know they must have been desperate because I felt a real fear for this woman's life. After we prayed for a few minutes the woman uttered a couple of sentences that came out in an odd, garbled fashion, her voice queerly masculine and unnatural. I continued to pray and when I finished we sat there under the cypress tree, just a gathering of women concerned for their sister. When she began to recover she was wiped out physically. We sat with her for an hour or so until she appeared to be recovered enough to walk home.

Shaista and I began the long walk back to our rendezvous point with the rest of the group so we could catch a ride back to the city. We walked along in silence for the first mile or so when she finally broke in. The people of Malawi didn't use my English name. They called me Chikhulupiriro, and that is how she addressed me.

"Chikhulupiriro, you heard the woman speak while we prayed over her? Would you like to know what she said?"

I was emotionally drained from the day's events and preferred the silence but I went ahead and answered. "What did she say?"

She said, "We must leave her and return to the water. He is in her now."

A shiver ran up my spine but I had my doubts about the implications. Other than that strange phrase the woman uttered I felt sure the woman had suffered a medical seizure of some sort. I knew without question that the entire episode was involuntary. It was not humanly possible to fake physical reactions to that extreme. My mind stumbled over itself and I fell silent, but Shaista continued. "This woman worked with the witch doctor."

"WITCH DOCTOR?" I asked, incredulous.

"Oh yes," she replied, "he is feared by many. This woman assisted him in casting spells."

I couldn't remark on her bizarre statement because I had no idea how I should respond. I just thanked Shaista for her help. My mind raced and I couldn't wait to get back to the guest house so I could meet with our team and ask for advice and guidance from the more mature and spiritually grounded people. I waited until everyone was seated around the table where we gathered every night to eat dinner. Everyone recounted the day's events in various locations throughout the countryside. The conversation buzzed because every experience had been different but exhilarating. When the conversation came around to me I sat at a table of fifteen people and feeling quite timid, I brought up the story of the woman in the water. The preacher was able to corroborate the part where she'd gone into convulsions but I was the only American present for the rest. When I concluded my story a couple of people sat there nonplussed, their mouths dropped open, but a few others reacted with incredulity.

"That's not biblically sound."

"Just a seizure, fairly common, no truth in that story."

They weren't mean, they just made it clear that the strange element of the story either didn't happen or I'd misinterpreted. I felt embarrassed and wished I hadn't even told the story to begin with. Of course they were right, I thought, I didn't even know for sure if spiritual possession was even compatible with their beliefs. I certainly didn't know anything about it, save from watching The Exorcist years before. After all the amazing things I'd witnessed in my short time there, I felt the doubt creeping back in again.

I went to my room, lay back on my bunk and stared up at the mosquito netting. Before long my roomie Lila came in. I shut off my music because after dinner we had a routine of studying in silence and afterward we'd have discussion together – usually the conversation centered on my need for reassurance that I was doing the right thing, that I was supposed to be there, etc. Lila was renowned in Malawi, having returned multiple times. She was well known and respected with the people and in sharp contrast to me; she conducted herself in an even-keeled, confident air of humble authority. It was very much like having my own mother's calming presence there to guide me.

Perhaps Lila sensed that even though I couldn't recite a litany of memorized scripture I was genuine in my motivations. That night she listened to my story again. She somehow knew just what I needed to hear. She didn't chastise me that what I'd witnessed was out of line with accepted doctrine. She didn't speak ill of those who doubted me. She simply assured me that I'd seen what I saw and done what I should, that is tried to help the woman and pray. Her words were all I needed to set my mind at ease. I fell asleep secure in the knowledge that my response amounted to the best I could give, and that had to be good enough. The next day would be our last day with the villagers. The day we would say goodbye. I wanted to be steady, calm and prepared to express to each and every one of them how they'd changed my life forever.

The final day was a wrapping up of sorts. We were slated to make one last visit to our adopted congregations, then gather for one last huge celebration at the Holy Dwelling Place in Lilongwe. Brother Johnny asked me to speak a few words of conclusion after which he would deliver his final sermon. As we sang and danced together in worship a line of church leaders filed up the center of the room. One of them was the choir director, Enoch. He'd admired my pink Nikes earlier in the week so I'd given them to him. I watched his pink sneakers shuffle up the aisle and my heart swelled. I wouldn't allow myself to get too emotional, however, because I'd prepared a special farewell for my friends. I noticed that Enoch looked different. He appeared glassy-eyed and in a daze. He made his way up to the front and then collapsed directly in front of me. He body convulsed in the exact manner as the woman from the day before, foam erupted from his mouth. His eyes jerked backward in their sockets. Several of the leaders carried Enoch outside and laid him on his back in the red dirt.

I knelt beside him much as I had the day before and what I saw appeared to be unbearable pain. I felt certain Enoch would die right there on the ground. His muscles tightened so that his limbs could not be moved. It appeared they might pop right out of his skin. He writhed and though he could not speak, a groan emerged from him. I tilted his chin upward the blue sky and once again attempted to clear

the airway. My composure that I'd worked so hard to

maintain abandoned me entirely. My body was wracked with

uninhibited sobs. Tears poured in rivers falling from me onto

Enoch's face and then running on to make little tracks in the

red dirt. I released my sorrow, pride, shame and despair right

there in one outpouring. The villagers looked on as they filed

out of the church to see what was happening.

Brother Johnny knelt next to me giving medical aid

and praying, all at the same time. After a long struggle, Enoch

regained consciousness. He acted confused, unaware of just

how he'd ended up flat on his back with a hysterical lady

dropping salty tears on his face. When he finally sat up, I sat

down on the ground. I felt drained and somewhat like a shell,

as though some kind of heavy weight had been expelled. It

was a good feeling. I was spent, but also some room had

been cleaned out, maybe a space that had been left collecting cobwebs and dust bunnies a little too long.

We re-entered the little church carrying Enoch. He wanted to stay and listen. Johnny asked me to go ahead and make my remarks. I was shocked he still wanted me to address the congregation given the emotional spectacle I'd made of myself. I'd written a speech the night before, nervous at the prospect of speaking to them and unsure of my ability to tell anyone how to seek out their own personal spiritual journey going forward. When I stood up in front of the people my fingers nervously felt for the spot in my Bible where I'd placed my written speech. But I never took it out. I began by thanking the people, explaining to them that I thought I'd come over to help them but instead they had helped and changed me. As I spoke my reticence vaporized and I felt a sense of boldness wash over; a feeling with which

I was unfamiliar in past public speaking events. My passion was evident as I spoke and the words seemed to propel themselves out of my mouth of their own accord. By the time I'd finished the people shouted and clapped. I promised them I would return. John walked up and whispered we had to leave; I'd spoken through all of my time, plus his time, too. We made our way out to the mini-bus and I felt a dread at the prospect of touching the door handle. I knew when I returned some of my friends would not be there. Some would inevitably be lost to malaria, simple infections, starvation. It's a shock when a child in the United States becomes ill and dies. In Malawi the loss of a child is not unusual, and the family is given three days to recover from the grief before they're expected by the village to get back to work.

By the time I returned to the United States I was

transformed. I never felt any particular need for material things before. But after I returned from Malawi I felt a compulsion to feel free of the weight of "things". I'd given everything away. I wanted to give my flip flops away, I wanted to come home naked, but someone said I might not be allowed on the airline without something on my feet. I felt light as air. I can say without question the closest I ever felt to spiritual ascendance was when I had nothing, not even my own name, and felt no compulsion to prove my worth to others. As long as I live I will never be able to give enough away to account for the love I've received. So tell me, now that I've been given so much and we've lived through this together ... what is it I can give to you?

Harvest

Now is the time of year when earth emerges from her great sleep. It is the time for buds and babies and little floating seeds dancing in the clouds. Now is the time when we witness the birth of the vintage.

Dad planted a little vineyard on our acre of land. He planned it carefully, conducting research on the perfect grape, able to withstand an extremely conflicted state like Oklahoma. The predictable part about our home is that nothing can reliably be predicted. For a decade now, Dad's grapes have survived successive droughts, great eighty-year floods, consecutive days of sub-zero cold in blizzard conditions and two straight months of triple digit heat.

He had to wait for two years before he could harvest even a single grape, yet he took his chair out to sit amongst the young vines. He swore he could see them growing before his very eyes. I've seen him panic and run around in circles, hands at his temples, during passing hailstorms. Watched he and my mother rush out to cover them with gunny sacks when they knew the weather forecast didn't call for a freeze. It happens to get a few degrees colder down here in the river valley than it does in the big city. He loves those vines. At first we couldn't understand it. This strange passion seemed to come out of nowhere, an unpredictable obsession set upon him well into his mid-forties, when a person ought to be thinking about the prospects of getting comfortable in ten years or so. Dad doesn't even drink wine, really, never has. Now, back in the day he was known to partake in his share of

Wild Turkey and cold beer, but he gave that up long ago (for the most part).

The plagues. Oh the plagues we've endured and come to expect in different forms every year. Bob Dylan wrote, *"behind everything beautiful there's been some kind of pain."* If that lyric is true then it is no wonder that vineyards are strikingly beautiful. The work of digging, planting and tending even the smallest vineyard is backbreaking, but it's the emotional pain that comes later that can knock you down.

The first plague arrived in the form of small Japanese beetles. You never predict the plague that's coming. One day you're out marveling at what you reckon might be the best harvest you've seen yet. You admire the low hanging clusters of gorgeous purple fruit, the juicy amethysts growing sweeter with each day in the sun. You begin to count down the days until Harvest arrives. The next day you go out only to find a squirming orgy of legs crawling over one another, reproducing and sucking all the juice from each grape. At times I've been away from home as Harvest nears and I always know as long as I don't hear anything from Dad, all is well. One year I'd taken my son to Disneyworld when I received a cryptic message: "small black spots on grapes. Black rot. Entire crop likely lost." Oklahoma received an uncommon amount of rain that summer, which made the vineyard vulnerable to a particularly rampant fungus. In my eternally optimistic tone I told him I would research it and find a way to get rid of it.

"There's nothing to be done," he explained. "It ruins the fruit and turns the grapes to mummies."

When I got back and looked at the fruit, sure enough, I found most of the grapes shriveled and hard as a stone. Not even worthy of raisin status.

Another year the birds descended. But the worst plague happened when the June Bugs came to town. When I was a little girl I'd go out in July and inspect the wild blackberry bushes. I loved the sweet taste of the berries and I popped them in my mouth by the handful under the hot sun. I also looked for June Bugs. I found them magical with their shiny green cases flashing in the sunlight. My friends said it was fun to tie a string around a June Bug's leg and let it fly around in circles. I couldn't do anything so cruel to such a lovely creature. I didn't mind sharing my blackberries with them. We had plenty for everyone.

But those little bastards ushered in a decided change

of heart when they set their winged sights on the vineyard. We'd watched the local weather and the meteorologist pointed out a scant cloud on the radar screen. "See that folks? That's not a thunderstorm. That, my friends, is a swarm of insects." Dad and I just looked at each other. We were just two weeks away from Harvest. The timing of Harvest is crucial because you want to bring in the fruit when the sugar and acid are at exact levels in the fruit. Harvesting too early results in too much acidity. Wait too long and you'll have dessert wine – a waste of time in our estimation.

The next evening Dad called and sounded resigned. The swarm of June Bugs had chosen the vineyard as their landing strip. He told me the speed with which they consumed the fruit was beyond belief.

"The entire crop will be gone in two days. I've

decided to just let it go."

"I'll be right there," I replied.

I drove to my parents' home that night. I woke up early next morning and wrapped my Neil Young bandana around my forehead. I was ready to go to war. Dad and I walked out and shook the vines. A great whirring cloud of green devils rose in the air. They seemed to recognize us as enemies. Never in my life did I expect to encounter an aggressive June Bug, but they went into attack mode, dive-bombing us, sometimes in swarms. If June Bugs had stingers I believe I'd be tits up in the pepper patch at this very moment. Still, we would not relent. I knew better than to try and drive every last one of them off, they weren't leaving until the final grape was drained. So we aimed to make Harvest early and save as much as we could. The whole family gathered to help. We worked all morning and through the afternoon. My sisters arrived in the afternoon, along with Mom and Philip. Working together we saved over half of the crop.

The processing time is crucial after the grapes are gathered in. It's necessary to de-stem and extract the juice for fermentation before the natural yeast begins to work the fruit on its own. After we bring the grapes in the family sits around in a circle and meticulously separates thousands of grapes from their stems by hand. Although this stage of the process may sound tedious, it is my favorite part. Music plays a crucial role at this point in the winemaking and our entire family takes turns picking songs*. There is no doubt the music infuses with the juice, you can't convince us otherwise. We have various Vintages of Hank, Leon, Bob and Neil. I've been known to pull an all-nighter in years past just to see that the entire crop is timely de-stemmed.

Then comes the most sublime aspect of viniculture. Just lately I've reached a better understanding regarding Dad's intent when he planted, cultivated and cared for those vines. It wasn't just for growing grapes. Every year after Dad presses the grapes and begins the fermentation process our entire family gathers together. Mom and Philip create a giant charcuterie plate with local cheeses and fruit, home grown peppers and onions. We serve it up with a bottle of vintage from the previous year. Grandma comes over to bring a homemade chocolate pie, though she chooses to abstain from the wine. The babies toddle over, curious to see what's bubbling in the buckets and the teenaged boys scuffle around.

Then we gather around the little table as one in the

modest house my parents have owned for forty years on the little plot of dirt where the spirit of our ancestors runs through our entwined hands. We stand in a circle and we pray. We pray to offer up gratitude, even on the years when the crop doesn't make. We give thanks for Barren Fork creek and the Illinois River, whose waters richen the stony terroir from which we bring in our Harvest. Every year, whether the crop is bountiful or scant, we offer up praise for the undying love we share and the bind it creates among us. It is a love that remains anchored to the ones who've already left us behind, so that we may live with the understanding our souls will someday reunite. We pray for strength to carry on in the way we have been taught and we pray for those who haven't found that kind of love yet. But there is one thing we never, ever pray for. And that is a June Bug.

"Behold, the days are coming, declares the Lord,

when the plowman shall overtake the reaper and the treader

of grapes him who sows the seed; the mountains shall drip

sweet wine, and all the hills shall flow with it. I will bring back

my exiled."

Exhibit D

Take Turns Playing Harvest Songs

1. Stranger in a Strange Land, Leon Russell
2. I Believe In You, Bob Dylan
3. After the Gold Rush, Neil Young
4. I Shall Be Released, The Band
5. Honey Bee, Tom Petty
6. The Log Train, Hank Williams, Sr.
7. Farmer's Daughter, Merle Haggard
8. The Mountain, Levon Helm
9. Precious and Grace, ZZ Top
10. Angel Flying Too Close to the Ground, Willie Nelson
11. Brothers In Arms, Dire Straits